THE TREASURE OF THE INCAS

THE FOULSHAM
HENTY LIBRARY

The Bravest of the Brave
In the Heart of the Rockies
The Treasure of the Incas
In the Reign of Terror
With Clive in India
With Wolfe in Canada

"I could find no bottom, Harry" he panted

THE FOULSHAM HENTY LIBRARY

THE
TREASURE OF THE
INCAS

A Story of Adventure in Peru

by

G. A. HENTY

LONDON
W. FOULSHAM & CO. LTD.
NEW YORK · TORONTO · CAPE TOWN · SYDNEY

This book has been carefully edited and slightly abridged to meet the reading tastes o the Modern Bo

MADE IN GREAT BRITAIN

by C. Tinling & Co. Ltd.
Liverpool, London and Presco

CONTENTS

CHAPTER I

HOW IT CAME ABOUT

Two men were sitting in the smoking-room of a London club. One of them was a man of sixty, the other some five- or six-and-twenty.

"I must do something," the younger man said, "for I have been kicking my heels about London since my ship was paid off two years ago. At first, of course, it didn't matter, for I have enough to live upon; but recently I have been fool enough to fall in love with a girl whose parents would never dream of allowing her to marry a half-pay lieutenant of the navy with no chance in the world of getting employed again."

"It is an awkward case certainly, Prendergast," the other said; "and though I sympathize with you, I cannot blame Fortescue. He is not what you might call a genial man, but there is no doubt that he was a splendid lawyer and a wonderful worker. I believe he would have gone on working till now had he not suddenly come in for a very fine estate. What his savings were I do not know, but they must be very large. His three sons are all at the bar, and are rising men, so there was no occasion for him to go on piling up money for them. But, as I say, he has always had the reputation of being a hard man, and it is practically certain that he would never allow his daughter to marry a man whom he would regard as next door to a pauper. Now, what are you thinking of doing?"

"Well, sir, Miss Fortescue has agreed to wait for me for two years, and of course I am eager to do something, but the question is what? I can sail a ship, but even could I get the command of a merchantman, it would not improve my position in the eyes of her parents. Now, you have been knocking about all over the world, I do wish you would give me your advice. Where is there money to be got? I am equally ready to go to the North Pole or the Equator."

"You talk Spanish, don't you?"

"Yes; all my service has been in the Mediterranean. We were two years off the coast of Spain, and in and out of its ports."

The elder man did not speak for a minute or two.

"You have not thought of South America?" he said at last.

"No, Mr. Barnett; I don't know that I have ever thought of one place more than another."

The other was again silent.

"I don't think you could do better anywhere," he said slowly. "It is a land with great possibilities. I was five years out there, and came home when the war broke out between Chile and the Spaniards. I have been more in Peru than in Chile, and as Peru was then still in the hands of the Spanish, it would have been impossible for me to go there again as long as the war lasted. Knocking about as I did, I heard a great deal from the natives (I mean the Indians). I gathered from them a number of their traditions, and I am convinced that they know of any number of gold mines that were formerly worked, but were blocked up when the Spaniards invaded the country, and have been kept secret ever since.

"The natives never spoke on the subject at all to the Spaniards. If they had, they would have been flogged until they revealed all they knew—that is to say, they would have been flogged to death, for no tortures will wring from an Indian anything he knows about gold. They look upon that metal as the source of all the misfortunes that have fallen upon their race. With an Englishman whom they knew and trusted, and who, as they also knew, had no wish whatever to discover gold mines, they were a little less reticent. I never asked them any questions on a subject in which I had not a shadow of interest, but I certainly had some curiosity, not of a pecuniary kind, because the matter had always been a riddle as to the hiding-place of the Incas' treasures. And from what I learned I should say it is absolutely certain that a great portion of these escaped the search of their Spanish tyrants. Now, of course, the Spaniards have been driven out.

"Whether the men who were employed in the work all died without revealing the secret, or whether it had been trusted to a chosen few, I know not; but the natives believe that there are still a few among them to whom the secret has been passed down from father to son. Anyhow, all had heard vague traditions. Some said that part of the treasure was carried hundreds of miles inland and given over to a tribe of fierce savages, in a country into which no European can enter. Another tradition is that a portion of it was carried off by sea in a great canoe, which was never heard of again and was believed to have been lost. I am not for a moment supposing, Prendergast, that if you went out there you would have the most remote chance of discovering what the Spaniards, ever since they landed there, tried in vain to find, and I certainly should not think of recommending a mad-brained adventure, but undoubtedly there are many rich gold mines yet to be found. There are openings for trade, too; and I can give you introductions to merchants both in Chile and Peru. It is not a thing I should recommend to everyone, far from it; but if you want to combine adventure with a chance, however small, of making money, I don't know that you can do better than go to

South America. You are fitted for no calling here; your income, counting your half-pay, would suffice to keep you out there, and a couple of years of such a life would do you no harm."

"It is just what I should like," the young man said enthusiastically.

"The thing would not be worth thinking of were it not that the man who always went with me as guide and muleteer is an Indian, and has, I am convinced, a knowledge of some of these places. He was with me all the time I was out there. I saved his life when a puma sprang upon him, and he more than once hinted that he could make me a rich man. On the chance that he is alive—and he was about thirty when he was with me fifteen years ago, so it is probable that he is still to the fore—I will give you a letter to him telling him that you are a friend of mine, and that I trust to him to do any service he can for you just as he would have done for myself.

"By the way, you mustn't think only of gold; silver is, after all, the chief source of the riches of Peru, and there are numbers of extraordinarily rich mines. It is calculated that three hundred millions have been produced since the first occupation by the Spaniards. Quicksilver is also very abundant; copper and lead are found too, but there is not much to be done with them at present, owing to the cost of carriage. There is good shooting in the mountains on the eastern side of the Andes, and you will find plenty of sport there."

They talked over the matter for some time before they separated, and Harry Prendergast became quite excited over it. On his return to his rooms he was astonished to find the candles alight and a strong smell of tobacco pervading the place. A lad of about sixteen leapt from the easy-chair in which he had been sitting.

"Hullo, Harry, I didn't expect you back so soon! The

maid said you were dining out, and I suppose that generally means one o'clock before you are back."

"Well, what brings you here, Bert? I thought I had got you off my hands for a year at least."

"I thought so, myself," the lad said coolly; "but circumstances have been too strong for me. We were running down the Channel the night before last, when a craft that was beating up ran smack into us. She knocked a hole in our side as big as a house, and we had just time to jump on board her. Our old craft went down two minutes after the skipper left her. It is a bad job, Harry, and I am horribly put out about it. Of course nothing could be saved, and there is all the new kit you bought for me down at the bottom. I shan't bother you again; I have quite made up my mind that I shall ship before the mast this time, and a five-pound note will buy me a good enough outfit for that."

"We need not talk about that now, Bertie. You are certainly an unlucky beggar; this is the second time you have been wrecked."

"It is a frightful nuisance," the boy said. "I am really awfully sorry, Harry. You have been a thundering good elder brother. I hated to think that you had to shell out last time, and I have quite made up my mind that you shan't do it again."

"Well, it cannot be helped; it is no fault of yours. Now shut your mouth altogether. I want to think."

They were silent for fully ten minutes, then Harry said:

"I told you about that business of mine with Miss Fortescue."

"Yes, you told me about it; an uncomfortable business, wasn't it?—surly old father, lovely daughter, and so on."

Harry said nothing for another five minutes.

"This is a serious matter," he said at last. "I am thinking of going way for two years."

The lad turned half round in his chair and had a good look at his brother.

"Where are you going to?" seeing by Harry's rather gloomy face that he was quite in earnest.

"I believe I am going to Peru. When I was talking at the club this evening to Mr. Barnett—you know that he is our oldest friend and is one of our trustees—I told him I was ready to do anything and go anywhere. Well, you know he was in Peru for some years. He says that the natives have all sorts of legends about rich mines that were hidden when the Spaniards came first, and that it is certain that, tremendous as was the amount of loot they got, a great part of the Incas' treasure was hidden away. Once or twice there had been great finds—in one case two million and a half dollars. It it believed that the secret is still known to certain Indians. When he went out there he had a muleteer, whose life he saved when he was attacked by some beast or other, and this man as much as hinted that he knew of a place where treasure might be concealed. Well, he offered to give me a letter to this man, and he regarded it as just possible that the fellow, who seems to be a descendant of some of the people who were members of the Incas' court at the time the Spaniards came, may have some knowledge of the rich mines that were then closed down, and that he may be able to show them to me, from his feeling of gratitude to Barnett. It is but one chance in a million, and as I can see no other possibility of making a fortune in two years, I am going to try it."

"Of course you will," the lad said excitedly, "and I should think that you would take me with you."

"I certainly had not dreamt of doing so, Bertie. But if I have to keep on getting fresh outfits for you, the idea has come into my mind during the last half-hour that I could not do better. The only doubt in my mind is whether it will be fair to you—you have got your profession."

"But I can go back to it if nothing good turns up, Harry. I can visit the firm and tell them that I am going to travel with you for a bit. I should think they would be rather glad, for they always build and never buy ships, and it will take them six months to replace the *Stella*. Besides, I shall pick up Spanish—at least, I suppose that is the language they speak out there—and shall learn no end of things. As you know, we trade with the west coast of America, so I should be a lot more useful to the firm when I come back than I am now."

"Well, I must think it over, and let you know in the morning. It will be a big expense, anyhow, and I don't mean, if possible, to draw upon my capital beyond three or four hundred pounds. I believe living is cheap out there. Of course I shall arrange for my income and half-pay to be sent out to some firm at Lima."

Harry Prendergast did not get much sleep that night. He blamed himself for having mentioned the matter at all to Bertie, and yet the more he thought over it the more he felt that it would be very pleasant to have his brother with him. If nothing came of it he would only have lost a couple of years, and, as the boy himself had said, the time would not have been altogether wasted. Bertie was down before him in the morning. He looked anxiously at his brother as he came in.

"Well, Harry?"

"Well, I have thought it over in every light. But in the first place, Bertie, if you go with me you will have to remember that I am you commanding officer. I am ten years older than you, and besides I am a lieutenant in the King's Navy, while you are only a midshipman in the merchant service. Now, I shall expect as ready obedience from you as if I were captain of my own ship and you one of my men; that is absolutely essential."

"Of course, Harry, it could not be otherwise."

"Very well, then; in the next place I shall abide by what Mr. Barnett says. He is your guardian as well as trustee, and has a perfect right to put a veto upon any wild expedition of this sort. Lastly, I should hope that you may get your employer's promise to take you back again in order that you may complete your time."

"I'll do my best, Harry!" the lad said gratefully.

"There is a good deal in what you say, Harry," Mr. Barnett said when Prendergast asked his opinion as to his taking his brother with him. "Two years would not make any material difference in his career as a sailor; it simply means that he will be so much older when he passes as mate. There is no harm in that. Everything considered, I think the idea of his going with you is a good one."

"I am glad you see it in that way, sir."

"I cannot advance any money out of the thousand pounds that will come to him when he is of age. By your father's will it was ordered that, in the event of his own death before that time, the interest was to accumulate. Your father foresaw that, like you, probably Bertie would take to the sea, and as the amount would be fully two thousand pounds by the time he comes of age, it would enable him to buy a share in any ship that he might, when he passed his last examination, command; but I will myself draw a cheque for a hundred pounds, which will help towards meeting expenses. I feel myself to some extent responsible for this expedition."

On returning to their lodgings Harry met his brother, who had been into the city.

"Old Prosser was very civil," said Bertie. "He said that

as their ships were chiefly in the South American trade it would be a great advantage for me to learn to speak Spanish well. They had not yet thought anything about whether they should order another ship to replace the *Stella;* at any rate, at present they had no vacancy, and would gladly give me permission to travel in South America, and would find me a berth to finish my apprenticeship when I returned. More than that, they said that as I had always been so favourably reported upon they would put me on as a supernumerary in the *Para,* which will sail in a fortnight for Callao. I should not draw pay, but I should be in their service, and the time would count, which would be a great pull, and I should get my passage for nothing."

"That is capital. Of course I will take a passage in her too."

The passage was arranged, and everything was made ready for the voyage. Harry said good-bye to Helen Fortescue, who promised to wait for him for two years.

The voyage was long but uneventful; and at last, just four months after leaving England, the brothers landed at Callao, on the coast of Peru. The next morning they set off on mules for the capital, Lima.

CHAPTER II

AT LIMA

It was six miles to Lima, but as the city is five hundred and twelve feet above the sea, the ascent was steady and somewhat steep. The road was desperately bad, and the country uninteresting, being for the most part dried up. As they neared the town vegetation became general, small canals irrigating the country. Here were fruit and vegetable gardens, with oranges, plantains, vines, and flowers.

Passing through a gate in the walls they entered the town. It could not be called imposing; the houses were low and irregular, fantastically painted in squares or stripes, and almost all had great balconies shut in with trellis-work. The hotel to which they had been recommended was a large building with a courtyard, with dining and other rooms opening from it, and above them the bedrooms. After settling themselves in their room they went out.

"We will wait until to-morrow before we begin what we may call business, Bertie," said Harry. "Of course I shall deliver the other letters of introduction that Mr. Barnett gave me; but the principal one—that to his former muleteer—is more important than all put together. If anything has happened to him, there is an end of any chance whatever of finding the treasure."

"I vote we go at once, Harry, and see if he is here."

"I don't think we shall find him here; for Barnett said that he lived in the village of Miraflores, five miles away on the north, and that if he is not there, Señor Pasquez, to whom I have a letter, will be likely to tell me where he is to be found, for he is often employed by him. As it is only eleven o'clock yet, there is no reason why we should not go to Miraflores."

They engaged two mules, and as the man of whom they hired them had a third, and he was ready to accompany them for a small fee, they agreed to take him with them.

Before they were a mile out of the town the mist cleared off and the sun shone brightly. The heat, however, was by no means too great to be pleasant. Miraflores was a charming village, or rather small town, nestling among gardens and orchards.

"I want to find a muleteer named Dias Otero," Harry said to their guide as they rode into the place.

"I know him well," he said. "Everyone about here knows Dias. His wife was a cousin of my mother's."

"Do you know whether he is at home now?"

"Yes, señor; I saw him in Lima three days ago. He had just come down from the mountains. He had been away two months, and certainly will not have started again so soon. Shall I lead you to his house at once?"

"Do so; it is to see him that I have come to this town."

"This is his house," the man said presently.

It lay in the outskirts of the town, and was neater than the generality of houses, and the garden was a mass of flowers. They dismounted, handed over the mules to their owner, and walked to the door. An Indian of some five-and-forty years came out as they did so.

"Are you Dias Otero?" Harry asked.

"The same, señor."

"I have just arrived from England, and bring a letter to you from Señor Barnett, with whom you travelled for two or three years some time ago."

The man's face lit up with pleasure. "Will you enter,

señor. Friends of Señor Barnett may command my services in any way. He once saved my life at the risk of his own. Is there any hope of his coming out again?"

"I do not think so, Dias. He is strong and well, but I do not think he is likely to start again on a journey of exploration. He is my greatest friend. My brother and I were left under his charge when we were young, and he has been almost a father to us. It is he who has sent us out to you. Here is his letter."

"Will you read it to me, señor. I cannot read; I am always obliged to get somebody to read my letters, and write answers for me."

The letter was of course in Spanish, and Harry read:

"Dear friend Dias,

"I am sending out to you a gentleman, Mr. Prendergast, an officer of the British Navy, in whom I am deeply interested. His brother accompanies him. I beg that you will treat them as you would me, and every service you can render him consider as rendered to myself. From a reason which he will no doubt explain to you in time, it is of the deepest importance to him that he should grow rich in the course of the next two years. He will place himself wholly in your hands. He does not care what danger he runs, or what hardships he has to go through in order to attain his purpose. I know that I need not say more to you. He has sufficient means to pay all expenses of travel for the time he will be out there. I know that you are descended from nobles of high rank at the court of the Incas when the Spaniards arrived, and that secrets known to but few were passed down from father to son in your family. If you can use any of those secrets to the advantage of my friend, I pray you most earnestly to do so. I trust that this letter will find you and your good wife in health. Had I been ten years younger I would have come out with my friends to aid them in their adventure, but I know that in putting them into your hands I shall be doing them a vastly greater service than I could do were I able to come in person."

When Harry ceased, the Indian sat for some time without speaking, then he said:

"It is a matter that I must think over, señor. It is a very grave one, and had any other man than Señor Barnett asked this service of me no money could have tempted me to assent to it. It is not only that my life would be in danger, but that my name would be held up to execration by all my people were I to divulge the secret that even the tortures of the Spaniards could not wring from us. I must think it over before I answer. It is a grave question, and it may be three or four days before I can decide."

"I thank you, Dias; but there is no occasion for you to give a final decision now. Whether or no, we shall travel for a while, and I trust that you will go with us with your mules and be our guide, as you did to Mr. Barnett. It will be time enough when you know us better to give us a final answer. Make arrangements for your mules and yourself for a three months' journey in the mountains, show us what there is to see of the gold and silver placers, and the quicksilver mines at Huanuco. At the end of that time you will know us and can say whether you are ready to aid us in our search."

The native bowed his head gravely.

"I will think it over," he said; "and now, señors, let us put that aside. My wife has been busy since you entered in preparing a simple meal, and I ask you to honour me by partaking of it."

"With pleasure, Dias."

It consisted of *puchero,* a stew consisting of a piece of

beef, cabbage, sweet-potatoes, salt pork, sausage-meat, pigs' feet, yuccas, bananas, quinces, pease, rice, salt, and an abundance of Chile peppers. This had been cooked for six hours and was now warmed up. Two bottles of excellent native wine, a flask of spirits, and some water were also put on the table. The Indian declined to sit down with them, saying that he had taken a meal an hour before.

While they ate he chatted with them, asking questions of their voyage and telling them of the state of things in the country.

"It is always the same, señors, there is a revolution and two or three battles; then either the president or the one who wants to be president escapes from the country or is taken and shot, and in a day or two there is a fresh pronunciamiento. We thought that when the Spaniards had been driven out we should have had peace, but it is not so."

"But does not this make travelling very unsafe?"

The Indian shrugged his shoulders.

"Peru is a large country, señor, and those who want to keep out of the way of the armies and fighting can do so; I myself have continued my occupation and have never fallen in with the armies. That is because the fighting is principally in the plains, or round Cuzco; for the men do not go into the mountains except as fugitives, as they could not find food there for an army. It is these fugitives who render the road somewhat unsafe; starving men must take what they can get. They do not interfere with the great silver convoys from Potosi or other mines—a loaf of bread is worth more than a bar of silver in the mountains—but they will plunder persons coming down with goods to the town or going up with their purchases. Once or twice I have had to give up the food I carried with me, but I have had little to grumble at, and I do not think you need trouble yourself about them; we will take care to avoid them as far as possible."

After chatting for an hour they left the cottage, and, mounting their mules, returned to Lima.

"I think he will help us, Harry," Bertie said as soon as they set out.

"I think so too, but we must not press him to begin with. Of course there is a question too as to how far he can help us. He may know vaguely where the rich mines once existed; but you must remember that they have been lost for three hundred years, and it may be impossible for even a man who has received the traditions as to their positions to hit upon the precise spot."

Next day they called on Señor Pasquez, who received them very cordially.

"So you are going to follow the example of Señor Barnett and spend some time in exploring the country and doing some shooting. Have you found Dias?"

"Yes, señor, and I think he will go with us, though he has not given a positive answer."

"You will be fortunate if you get him. He can give you much useful advice; he knows exactly what you will have to take with you, the best districts to visit for your purpose, and the best way of getting there. For the rest, I shall be very happy to take charge of any money you may wish to leave behind, and to act as your banker and cash any orders you may draw upon me. I will also receive and place to your account any sums that may be sent you from England."

"That, sir, is a matter which Mr. Barnett advised me to place in your hands. After making what few purchases we require, and taking fifty pounds in silver, I shall have two hundred and fifty pounds to place in your hands. Mr. Barnett will manage my affairs in my absence, and will send to you fifty pounds quarterly."

"You will find difficulty in spending it all in two years," the merchant said with a smile. "If you are content to live on what can be bought in the country, it costs very little; and as for the mules, they can generally pick up enough at their halting-places to serve them, with a small allowance of grain. You can hire them cheaply, or you can buy them. The latter is cheaper in the end, but you cannot be sure of getting mules accustomed to mountains, and you would therefore run the risk of their losing their foothold, and not only being dashed to pieces but destroying their saddles and loads. However, if you secure the services of Dias Otero, you will get mules that know every path in the mountains."

Next day Dias came to the hotel.

"I have thought it over, señor," he said. "I wish, before making any arrangement, that the matter should be thoroughly understood. I have no certain knowledge whatever as to any of the lost mines, still less of any hidden treasures; but I know all the traditions that have passed down concerning them. I doubt whether any Indians now possess a certain knowledge of these things. For generations, no doubt, the secrets were handed down from father to son, and it is possible that some few may still know of these places; but I doubt it. Few now can know more than I do, yet I am sure of nothing. I know generally where the mines were situated and where some treasures were concealed, and what knowledge I have I will place at your service; but so great a care was used in the concealment of the entrances to the mines, so carefully were the hiding-places of the treasures chosen, and so cunningly concealed, that, without the surest indications and the most minute instructions, we might search for years, as men indeed have done ever since the Spanish came here, without finding them. I am glad that I can lay my hand upon my heart and say, that whatever may have been possessed by ancestors of mine, no actual details have ever come down to me; for, had it been so, I could not have revealed them to you. We know that all who were instructed in these were bound by the most terrible oaths not to reveal them. Numbers have died under the torture rather than break those oaths; and even now, were one of us to betray the secrets that had come down to him, he would be regarded as accursed. No one would break bread with him, every door would be closed against him, and if he died his body would rot where it fell. But my knowledge is merely general, gathered not only from the traditions known to all our people, but from confidences made by one member of our family to another. Full knowledge was undoubtedly given to some of them; but all these must have died without initiating others into the full particulars. Such knowledge as I have is at your disposal. I can take you to the localities, I can say to you, 'Near this place was a great mine,' but unless chance favours you you may search in vain."

"That is quite as much as I had hoped for, Dias, and I am grateful for your willingness to do what you can for us, just as you did for Señor Barnett."

CHAPTER III

A STREET FRAY

"Now, señor," Dias said, "as we have settled the main point, let us talk over the arrangements. What is the weight of your baggage?"

"Not more than a mule could carry. Of course we shall sling our rifles over our shoulders. We have a good stock of ammunition for them and for our pistols. We shall each take two suits of clothes besides those we wear, and a case of spirits in the event of accident or illness. We should, of course, require a few cooking utensils, tin plates, mugs, and cups. What should we need besides these?"

"A tent and bedding, señor. We should only have, at the start, to carry such provisions as we could not buy. When we are beyond the range of villages in the forests we might often be weeks without being able to buy anything; still, we should probably be able to shoot game for food. We should find fruits, but flour we shall have to take with us from the last town we pass through before we strike into the mountains, and dried meat for an emergency; and it would be well to have a bag of grain, so that we could give a handful or so to each of the mules. I am glad you have brought some good spirits—we shall need it in the swamps by the rivers. Your tea and coffee will save your having to buy them here, but you will want some sugar. We must take two picks and a shovel, a hammer for breaking up ore, a small furnace, twenty crucibles and bellows, and a few other things for aiding to melt the ore. You would want for the journey five baggage mules, and, of course, three riding mules. I could hardly manage them, even with aid from you, in very bad places, and I would rather not take any strange man with me on such business as we have in hand. But some assistance I must have, and I will take with me my nephew José. He has lost his father, and I have taken him as my assistant, and shall train him to be a guide such as I am. He is but fifteen, but he already knows something of his business."

"That would certainly be far better than having a muleteer whom you could not trust, Dias. Now, how about the eight mules?"

"I have five of my own, as good mules as are to be found in the province; we shall have to buy the three others for riding."

"But you will want four for riding."

"No, señor; yours and the one I ride will be enough. José at times will take my place, and can when he likes perch on one of the most lightly laden animals."

"How much will the riding mules cost?"

"I can get fair ones for about fifty dollars apiece; trade is slack at present owing to the troubles, and there are many who would be glad to get rid of one or two of their train."

"And now, Dias, we come to the very important question, what are we to pay you for yourself, your nephew, and the five mules—say by the month?"

"I have been thinking the matter over, señor—I have talked it over with my wife"—he paused for a moment, and then said: "She wishes very much to go with me, señor."

Harry opened his eyes in surprise. "But surely, Dias, you could not think of taking her on such an expedition, where, as you say yourself, you may meet with many grave dangers and difficulties?"

"A woman can support them as well as a man," Dias said quietly. "My wife has more than once accompanied me on journeys when I have been working on contract. We have been married for fifteen years, and she has no children to keep her at home. She is accustomed to my being away for weeks. This would be for months, perhaps for two years. At first she tried to dissuade me from going for so long a time; but when I told her that you were sent me by the gentleman who saved my life a year after I married her, she agreed at once that it was my duty to go, and she prayed me to take her with me. I said that I would put it before you, señor, and that I must abide by your decision."

"By all means bring her with you, Dias. If you and she are both willing to share the dangers we should meet with, surely we cannot object in any way."

"Thank you, señor. She will ride behind me on my mule. You have already seen that she can cook well; and if we have José to look after the animals when we are searching among the hills, you will find it not unpleasant, when we return of an evening, to find a hot supper ready for us."

"That is quite true, and I am sure we shall find your wife a great acquisition to our party. And now about payment?"

"I shall not overcharge you," Dias said with a smile. "You will remember, señor, that I make this journey not as a business matter—no money would buy from me any information that I may have as to hidden mines or treasures—I do it to repay a debt of gratitude to my preserver, Don Henry Barnett, and partly because I am sure that I shall like you and your brother as I did him. I shall aid you as far as lies in my power in the object for which you are undertaking this journey. Therefore until it is finished there shall be no talk about payment. If we meet with no success, and return to Lima empty-handed, I shall have lost nothing. I shall have had no expenses at home, my wife and I will have fed at your expense, and José will have learned so much that he would be as good a guide as any in the country. You could then give me the three mules you will buy, to take the place of any of mine that may have perished on the journey, and should you have them to spare, I will take a hundred dollars as a *bueno mano*. If we succeed, and you discover a rich mine or a hidden treasure, you shall then pay me what it pleases you. Is it a bargain?"

"The bargain you propose is ridiculously one-sided, Dias, and I don't see how I could possibly accept the offer you make to me."

"Those are my terms señor," Dias said simply, "to take or to leave."

"Then I cannot but accept them, and I thank you most heartily"; and he held out his hand to Dias, and the Indian grasped it warmly.

"When do you propose we shall start?"

"Will this day week suit you, señor? There are the mules to buy, and the tents to be made—they should be of vicuña skin with the wool still on, which, with the leather kept well oiled, will keep out water. Then I shall have five leather bags made to hold the beds and blankets. But the making of the beds and tents will take some time —people do not hurry in Lima—and there will be the riding saddles and bridles to get, and the provisions. I do not think we can be ready before another week. It will be well, then, that you should, before starting away, visit the ruins of Pachacamac. All travellers go there, and it will seem only natural that you should do so, for there you will see the style of the buildings, and also the explorations that were everywhere made by the Spaniards in search of treasure."

"Very well, Dias; then this day week we shall be ready to start."

Three days later Dias said he thought they might as well start the next day to Pachacamac.

"We shall only want the three riding mules and one for baggage. Of course we shall not take José or my wife. By the time we return everything will be ready for us."

"I shall be very glad to be off, Dias. We know no one here except Señor Pasquez; and although he has been very civil and has begged us to consider his house as our own, he is of course busy during the day, and one can't do above a certain amount of walking about the streets. So by all means let us start tomorrow morning."

Starting at sunrise, they rode for some distance through a fertile valley, and then crossed a sandy plain until they reached the little valley of Lurin, in which stand the ruins of Pachacamac. This was the sacred city of the natives of the coast before their conquest by the Incas. During their forty-mile ride Dias told them something of the place they were about to visit. Pachacamac, meaning "the creator of the world", was the chief divinity of these early people, and here was the great temple dedicated to him. The Incas after their conquest erected a vast Temple of the Sun, but they did not attempt to suppress the worship of Pachacamac, and the two flourished side by side until the arrival of the Spaniards. The wealth of the temple was great; the Spaniards carried away among their spoils one thousand six hundred and eighty-seven pounds of gold and one thousand six hundred ounces of silver; but with all their efforts they failed to discover the main treasure, said to have been no less than twenty-four thousand eight hundred pounds of gold, which had been carried away and buried before their arrival. Tradition has it that it was buried somewhere between this town and Lima. Doubtless all concerned in the matter fled before the Spaniards arrived, at any rate with all their cruelty the invaders never discovered its position. The report that it was buried near may have been set about to prevent their hunting for it elsewhere, and the gold may be lying now somewhere in the heart of the mountains."

Harry Prendergast and his brother looked in astonishment at the massive walls that rose around the eminence on which the temple had stood. The latter had disappeared, but its situation could be traced on the plateau buttressed by the walls. These were of immense thickness, and formed of huge adobe bricks almost as hard as stone; even the long efforts of the Spaniards had caused but little damage to them. The plateau rose some five hundred feet above the sea, which almost washed one face of it. Half-way up the hill four series of these massive walls, whose tops formed terraces, stood in giant steps some fifty feet high. Here and there spots of red paint could be seen, showing that the whole surface was originally painted. The ascent was made by winding passages through the walls. On the side of the upper area facing the sea could be seen the remains of a sort of walk or esplanade, with traces of edifices of various kinds.

Pachacamac was the most sacred spot in South America, vast numbers of pilgrims came here from all points. The city itself had entirely disappeared, covered deeply in sand, but for a long distance round, it had, like the neighbourhood of Jerusalem and Mecca, been a vast cemetery, and a small amount of excavation showed the tombs of the faithful, occupied in most cases by mummies.

"We will ride across to the Incas' temple. There is not much to see there, but it is as well that you should look at the vaults in which the treasures were hid. There are similar places at Cuzco and several of the other ruins."

"It may certainly be useful to see them," Harry agreed,

and they rode across the plain. Leaving their mules outside they entered the ruins. The Indian led them into some underground chambers. He had brought a torch with him, and this he now lit.

"You have to be careful or you might otherwise tumble into one of these holes and break a limb; and in that case, if you were here by yourselves, you would certainly never get out again."

They came upon several of these places. The openings were sometimes square and sometimes circular, and had doubtless been covered with square stones. They were dug out of the solid ground. For about six feet the sides of the pit were perpendicular; in some it swelled out like a great vase with a broad shoulder, in others it became a square chamber of some size.

"Some of these places were no doubt meant to store grain and other provisions," the Indian said, "some were undoubtedly treasuries."

"Awkward places to find," Harry said; "one might spend a lifetime in searching for them in only one of these temples."

"They were the last places we should think of searching," Dias said. "For years the Spaniards kept thousands of men at work. I do not say that there may not be some few places that have escaped the searchers, but what they could not with their host of workers find certainly could not be found by four or five men. It is not in the temples that the Incas' wealth has been hidden, but in caves, in deep mountain gorges, and possibly in ruins on the other side of the mountains where even the Spaniards never penetrated. There are such places. I know of one to which I will take you if our search fails elsewhere. It is near the sea, and yet there are not half a dozen living men who have ever seen it, so strangely is it hidden. Tradition says that it was not the work of the Incas, but of the people before them. I have never seen it close. It is guarded, they say, by demons, and no native would go within miles of it. The traditions are that the Incas, when they conquered the land, found the place and searched it, after starving out the native chief who had fled there with his followers and family. Some say that they found great treasure there, others that they discovered nothing; all agree that a pestilence carried off nearly all those who had captured it. Others went, and they too died, and the place was abandoned as accursed, and in time its very existence became forgotten; though some say that members of the tribe have always kept watch there, and that those who carelessly or curiously approached it have always met with their death in strange ways. Although I am a Christian, and have been taught to disbelieve the superstitions of my countrymen, I would not enter it on any condition."

"If we happen to be near it I shall certainly take a close look at it," Harry said with a laugh. "I don't fancy we should see anything that our rifles and pistols would find invulnerable."

It was getting dark by the time they had finished their inspection of the rooms, so, riding two or three miles away, they encamped in a grove up the valley. Next morning they returned to Lima. Dias had given out that the two white señors intended to visit all the ruined temples of the Incas, and as other travellers had done the same their intention excited neither surprise nor comment.

On the following evening after dark Harry and his brother were returning from the house of Señor Pasquez.

"It is a pleasant house," Harry said; "the girls are pretty and nice, they play and sing well, and are really charming."

Bertie was about to answer, when there was an outburst

of shouts from a wine-shop they were passing, and in a moment the door burst open and half a dozen men engaged in a fierce conflict rushed out. Knives were flashing, and it was evident that one man was being attacked by the rest. By the light that streamed out of the open door they saw that the man attacked was Dias. It flashed across Harry's mind that if this man was killed there was an end to all hope of success in their expedition.

With a shout he sprang forward and struck to the ground a man who was dodging behind Dias with uplifted knife, while Bertie leapt on to the back of another, the shock throwing the man down face forward. Bertie was on his feet in a moment, and brought the stick he carried with all his force down on the man's head as he tried to rise. Then, springing forward again, he struck another man a heavy blow on the wrist. The knife dropped from the man's hand, and as he dashed with a fierce oath upon Bertie the stick descended again, this time on his head, and felled him to the ground. In the meantime one of the assailants had turned fiercely on Harry and aimed a blow at him with his knife; but with the ease of a practised boxer Harry stepped back, and before the man could again raise the knife he leaped in and struck him a tremendous blow on the point of his chin. The fifth man took to his heels immediately. The other four lay where they had fallen, evidently fearing they would be stabbed should they try to get on to their feet.

"Are you hurt, Dias?" Harry exclaimed.

"I have several cuts, señor, but none of them, I think, serious. You have saved my life."

"Never mind that now, Dias. What shall we do with these fellows—hand them over to the watch?"

"No, señor, that would be the last thing to do; we might be detained here for months. I will take all their knives and let them go."

"Here are two of them," Bertie said, picking up those of the men he had struck.

Dias stood over the man Harry had first knocked down, and with a fierce whisper ordered him to give up his knife, which he did at once. The other was still stupid from the effect of the blow and his fall, and Dias had only to take his knife from his relaxed fingers.

"Now, señor, let us be going before anyone comes along."

"What was it all about, Dias," Harry asked as he walked away.

"Many of the muleteers are jealous, señor, because I always get what they consider the best jobs. I had gone into the wine-shop for a glass of pulque before going round to see that the mules were all right. As I was drinking, these men whispered together, and then one came up to me and began to abuse me, and directly I answered him the whole of them drew their knives and rushed at me. I was ready too, and wounded two of them as I fought my way to the door. As I opened it one of them stabbed me in the shoulder, but it was a slanting blow. Once out they all attacked me at once, and in another minute you would have had to look for another muleteer. 'Tis strange, señors, that you should have saved my life as Mr. Barnett did. It was a great deed to risk your lives with no weapons but your sticks against five ruffians with their knives."

"I did not use my stick," Harry said. "I am more accustomed to use my fists than a stick, and can hit as hard with them, as you saw. But my brother's stick turned out the most useful. He can box too, but cannot give as heavy a blow as I can. Still, it was very lucky that I followed your advice, and bought a couple of heavy sticks to carry with us if we should go out after dark.

Now you had better come to the hotel, and I will send for a surgeon to dress your wound."

"It is not necessary, señor; my wife is waiting for me in my room, she arrived this afternoon. Knife cuts are not uncommon affairs here, and she knows quite enough to be able to bandage them."

"At any rate we shall have to put off our start for a few days."

"Not at all, señor; a bandage tonight and a few strips of plaster in the morning will do the business. I shall be stiff for a few days, but that will not interfere with my riding, and José will be able to load and unload the mules, if you will give him a little assistance. Adios! and a thousand thanks."

Next morning Dias and his wife came up early. The former had one arm in a sling. As they entered, the woman ran forward, and, throwing her arms round Bertie, she kissed him on both cheeks. The lad was too much surprised at this unexpected salute to return it, as his brother did when she did the same to him. Then, drawing back, she poured out her thanks volubly, the tears running down her cheeks.

"Maria asked me if she might kiss you," Dias said gravely when she stopped. "I said that it was right that she should do so, for do we not both owe you my life?"

"You must not make too much of the affair, Dias; four blows were struck, and there was an end to it."

"A small matter to you, señor, but a great one to us."

"You don't think those rascals are likely to waylay us on the road, and take their revenge?"

"Not they, señor. The matter is settled. They have not been seriously hurt. Except the two hurt in the wine-shop they will not even have a scar to remind them of it. In two years they will have other things to think about, if it is true that Colombia means to go to war with Chile."

"What is the quarrel about, Dias?"

"The Colombians helped us to get rid of the Spaniards, but ever since they have presumed a right to manage affairs here."

"Perhaps nothing will come of it."

"Well, it is quite certain that there is no very good feeling between Chile, Bolivia, Colombia, and Peru."

"I suppose they will be fighting all round some day?"

"Yes, and it will interfere with my business. Certainly we are better off than when the Spaniards were here; but the taxes are heavy, and things don't go as people expected they would when we got rid of the Spaniards. All the governments seem jealous of each other. I don't take any interest in these matters except so far as they interfere with trade. If every man would attend to his own affairs it would be better for us all."

CHAPTER IV

AMONG THE MOUNTAINS

Two days later the mules were brought round to the door at sunrise, and Harry and his brother sallied out from the hotel dressed for the first time in Peruvian costume. They were both warmly clothed. On their heads were felt hats with broad brims, which could be pulled down and tied over the ears, both for warmth and to prevent their being blown away by the fierce winds that sweep down the gorges. A thick poncho of llama wool fell from their shoulders to their knees, and loosely tied round their necks were thick and brightly-coloured scarves. They wore high boots, and carried large knives stuck in a strap below the knee. The rifles were fastened at the bow of their saddles, and their wallets, with provisions for the day, were strapped behind. By the advice of Dias each had in his pocket a large pair of green goggles, to protect their eyes from the glare of sun and snow.

They had spent the previous afternoon in packing the bundles, in which every item was put away so that it could be got at readily, and in making sure that nothing had been omitted. The five baggage mules were fastened one behind another, and José stood at the head of the leading one. As they came out Dias swung his wife on to a cushion strapped behind his saddle, and mounted himself before her. Harry and his brother climbed into theirs. They had both refused to put on the heavy and cruel spurs worn by the Peruvians, but had, at the earnest request of the Indian, put them in their saddle-bags.

"You will want them," he said. "You need not use them cruelly, but you must give your mules an occasional prick to let them know that you have spurs."

On leaving the town the road ran up the valley of the Rimac, a small river, but of vital importance to the country through which it passes, as small canals branching from it irrigate the land.

"The Spaniards have done some good here at least," Harry said to Dias, who was riding beside him.

"Some of these canals were constructed in their time, but the rest existed long before they came here, and, indeed, long before the Incas came. The Incas' work lies chiefly beyond the mountains; on this side almost all the great ruins are of cities and fortresses built by the old people. Cuzco was the Incas' capital, and almost all the towns between the two ranges of the Andes were their work. It is true that they conquered the people down to the sea, but they do not seem to have cared to live here. The treasures of Pachacamac and the other places on the plains were those of the old people and the old religion. The inhabitants of the plains are for the most part descendants of those people. The Incas were strong and powerful, but they were not numerous. That was why the Spaniards conquered them so easily. The old people, who regarded them as their masters, did not care to fight for them, just as the Peruvians did not care to fight for the Spaniards."

Five miles from Lima they passed through the little village of Quiraz. Beyond this they came upon many cotton plantations, and in the ravines by the side of the valley or among the ruins of Indian towns were several large fortresses. They also passed the remains of an old Spanish town and several haciendas, where many cattle and horses were grazing. They were ascending steadily, and after passing Santa Clara, eleven miles from Lima, the valley narrowed and became little more than a ravine. On either side were rents made in the hills by earthquakes, and immense boulders and stones were scattered about at the bottom of the narrow gorge. Four hours' travelling brought them to Chosica, where the valley widened again near the foot of the hills.

Here they halted for the day. There was an inn here which Dias assured them was clean and comfortable, and they therefore took a couple of rooms for the night in preference to unpacking their tents.

"It is just as well not to begin that till we get farther away," Harry said. "We have met any number of laden mules coming down, and if we were to camp here we should cause general curiosity."

He accordingly ordered dinner for himself and his brother, Dias preferring to take his meal in a large room used by passing muleteers. The fare was as good as they had had at the hotel at Lima.

There were still four hours of daylight after they had finished their meal, so they went out with Dias to explore one of the numerous burying-grounds round the village. It consisted of sunken chambers. In these were bones, with remains of the mats in which the bodies had been clothed. These wrappings resembled small sacks, and they remarked that the people must have been of very small size, or they could never have been packed away in them. With them had been buried many of the implements of their trade. One or two had apparently not been opened. Here were knitting utensils, toilet articles, implements for weaving, spools of thread, needles of bone and bronze. With the body of a girl had been placed a kind of work-box, containing the articles that she had used, and the mummy of a parrot, some beads, and fragments of an ornament of silver. Dias told them that all these tombs were made long before the coming of the

Incas. He said that round the heads of the men and boys were wound the slings they had used in life, while a piece of cotton flock was wrapped round the heads of the women. Many of the graves communicated with each other by very narrow passages; the purpose of these was not clear, but probably they were made to enable the spirits of the dead to meet and hold communion with each other.

"I don't want to see any more of them," Bertie said after they had spent three hours in their investigations; "this sort of thing is enough to give one a fit of the blues."

Beyond Chosica civilisation almost ceased. The road became little more than a mule track, and was in many places almost impassable by vehicles of any kind. Nothing could be wilder than the scenery they passed. At times rivers ran through perpendicular gorges, and the track wound up and down steep ravines. Sometimes they would all dismount, though Dias assured them it was not necessary; still, it made a change from the monotonous pace of little over two miles an hour at which the mules breasted the steep incline.

There were villages every few miles, but now when they halted they did so as a rule a mile before they got to one of these. Dinner was cooked over a fire of dead sticks, and after the meal Harry's tent was erected and the bed spread in it. The Indians went on to the village for the night, while Harry and his brother sat and smoked for a time by the fire and then turned in. At daybreak Dias rode back leading their riding mules and a baggage animal; the tent, beds, and the cooking utensils were packed up, and they rode in to the village and passed on at a trot until they overtook Maria and José, who had started with the other four mules when Dias rode away. At last they reached the head of the pass, and two days' journey took them to Oroya, standing on an elevated plateau some ten thousand feet above the sea, and five thousand below the highest point of the road.

The scenery had now completely changed. Villages were scattered thickly over the plain, cultivation was general. The hillsides were lined by artificial terraces, on which were perched chalets and small hamlets—they had seen similar terraces on the way up. These were as the Spaniards found them, and must at one time have been inhabited by a thriving population. Even now gardens and orchards flourished upon them up to the highest points on the hills. Oroya was a large place, and, avoiding the busy part of the town, they hired rooms, as it was necessary to give the mules two days' rest. On the first evening after their arrival they gathered round a fire, for the nights were cold, and even in the daytime they did not find their numerous wraps too hot for them.

"Now, Dias," Harry said, "we must talk over our plans. You said that we would not decide upon anything till we got here."

"I have been thinking it over deeply," Dias said. "First as to mines; at present almost all the gold that is obtained is acquired by washing the sands of rivers. Here and there gold has been found in rocks, but not in sufficient quantities to make mining pay. The rivers whose sands are richest in gold are in the mountains that lie behind Lake Titicaca, which lies to the south of Cuzco and on the border of Bolivia. No one doubts that in the time of the Incas there existed gold mines, and very rich ones; for if it had not been so it is impossible to account for the enormous amount of gold obtained by the Spanish conquerors, and no one doubts that they got but a small portion of the gold in existence when they arrived. It is of no use whatever for us to search the old ruins of the Incas in Cuzco, or their other great towns; all that can be found there has already been carried away.

"Now you see, señor, Huanuco, Jauja, Cuzco, and Puno all lie near the eastern range of the Andes, and when the alarm caused by the arrogant conduct of the Spaniards began, it was natural that the treasures should be sent away into the heart of those mountains. The towns on the western sides of this plateau, Challhuanca, Tanibobamba, Huancavelica, would as naturally send theirs for safety into the gorges of the western Andes, but all traditions point to the fact that this was not done by the Incas. As soon as the Spaniards arrived and struck the first blow, the great chiefs would naturally call together a band of their followers on whose fidelity they could rely, load the treasures on llamas, of which they possessed great numbers, and hurry them off to the mountains.

"It is among the mountains, therefore, that our search must be made. All our traditions point to the fact that it was along the eastern range of the Cordilleras, and the country beyond, that by far the greater portion of the treasures were taken for concealment. At any rate, as we have but eighteen months for the search it is on that side that we must try, and ten times that length of time would be insufficient for us to do it thoroughly. As to the gold mines, it is certain that they lie in that portion of the range between Cuzco and Lake Titicaca. It was near Puno, a short distance from the lake, that the Spaniards, owing to the folly of an Indian, found great treasures in a cave. They would probably have found much more had not a stream suddenly burst out which flooded the whole valley and converted it into a lake. Which do you think we had better look for first, gold mines or hidden treasures?"

"Of course that must depend on you, Dias, and how much you know about these matters. I need not say that a hidden treasure would be of vastly more use to me than the richest gold mine in the world. To obtain the gold from a mine an abundance of labour is required, besides machinery for crushing quartz and separating the gold from it. In the bed of a river, if it is rich and abounding in nuggets, three or four men, with rough machinery, could wash out a large quantity of gold in a short time, and a place of that sort would be far better than a rich mine, which could not be worked without a large amount of capital."

"I have heard tales of such places on the other side of the mountains to the south. From time to time gold-seekers have returned with as much as they could carry, but not one in a hundred of those that go ever come back; some doubtless die from hunger and hardship, but more are killed by the Indians. Most of the tribes there are extremely savage, and are constantly at war with each other, and they slay every white man who ventures into their country."

"Then is it not probable, Dias, that the gold could have come from their country?"

"Not from the plains, but from the streams running down into them; and although the Incas never attempted to subdue the tribes beyond the mountains, they may have had bodies of troops to protect the workers from incursions by these savages."

"Are there many wild beasts there?"

"In some parts of the mountains pumas and jaguars abound."

"That is not altogether satisfactory, though I should not mind if we fell in with one occasionally. But how about game, Dias?"

"The chief game are the wild vicuñas, which are very numerous in some parts; but they are very shy and difficult to hunt. Deer are plentiful, and there are foxes, bears, and hogs; but the great article of food is fish. On the plains the manatee, which is very like the seal, is caught; turtles are found in great numbers, and the people make oil from their eggs; and the buffo, a sort of porpoise, also abounds. The natives do not eat these, except when very pressed for food; they catch them for the sake of their oil. There are many kinds of fish: the sunaro, which I heard an English traveller say are like the fish the English call the pike; these grow to the length of seven or eight feet. And many smaller kinds of fish are caught by throwing the juice of the root of the barbasto into small streams. This makes the fish stupid, and they float on the surface so that they may easily be caught by hand. There are also many sorts of fruit."

"Well, then, we ought to do fairly well, Dias."

"Yes, señor; but many of these creatures are only found in the forests and in the rivers of the plains, and they are so much hunted by the savages there that they are very shy. But there are some creatures with which we certainly do not wish to meet, and unfortunately these are not uncommon. I mean the alligators and the great serpents. The natives fear the alligators much, for their weapons are of no avail against them, and they would never venture to attack a great snake."

"And besides these, what other disagreeables are there, Dias?" Bertie asked cheerfully."

"There is one other disagreeable," Dias replied, "and it is a serious one. There are in the mountains many desperate men. Some have slain an enemy who had friends influential enough to set the law in motion against them, or have escaped from prison; some have resisted the tax-collectors; many have been suspected of plotting against the government; and others are too lazy to work."

"And how do they live?" Harry asked.

"They live partly on game and partly on plunder. They steal from cultivators; they are paid a small sum by all muleteers passing through the mountains; they rob travellers who are worth robbing; and sometimes they carry off a proprietor of land, and get a ransom for him. Occasionally they will wash the sand, and get gold enough to send one of their number into a town to buy articles they require."

"And do they go in large bands?"

"No, señor; as a rule some ten or twelve keep together under the one they have chosen as their chief. Sometimes, if people make complaints and troops are sent against them, they will join to resist them; but this is not often. The authorities know well enough that they have no chance of catching these men among the mountains they are so well acquainted with, and content themselves with stationing a few troops in the villages."

"Have you fallen in with them often, Dias?"

"Yes; but, as you see, they have done me no harm. Sometimes, when I get to the end of my journey, the mules are not so heavily laden as when I started; but generally the people for whom I work say to me, 'Here are so many dollars, Dias; they are for toll.' There are places in the villages at the foot of the most-frequented passes where it is understood that a payment of so many dollars per mule will enable you to pass without molestation. In return for your money, you receive a ribbon, or a rosette, or a feather, and this you place in your hat as a passport. You may meet a few men with guns as you pass along, but when they see the sign they salute you civilly, ask for a drink of wine if you are carrying it, then wish you good-day. It is only in little-frequented passes that you have to take your chance. I may say that though these men may plunder, they never kill a muleteer. They know that if they did, all traffic on the road would cease, and the soldiers would find guides who knew every path and hiding-place in the mountains. Still, I hope we shall not be troubled with them, or with the Indians. You see, it is not so much an attack by day that we have to fear, as a surprise at night. Of course, when we are once on the hills, José and I will keep watch by turns. He is as sharp as a needle. I should have no fear of any of these robbers creeping up on us without his hearing them. But I can't say so much for him in the case of the Indians, who can move so noiselessly that even a vicuña would not hear them until they were within a spear's-throw."

"The spear is their weapon then, Dias?"

"Some tribes carry bows and arrows, others only spears, and sometimes they poison the points of both these weapons."

"That is unpleasant. Are there remedies for the poisons?"

"None that I know of, nor do I think the savages themselves know of any. The only chance is to pour ammonia at once into the hole that is made by an arrow, and to cut out all the flesh round a spear-wound, and then to pour in ammonia or sear it with a hot iron."

"That accounts for your buying that large bottle of ammonia at Lima. I wondered what you wanted it for. When we get into the country these unpleasant people inhabit, I will fill my spirit-flask with it, so that it will always be handy if required. Now we understand things generally, Dias. It only remains for you to decide where we had best leave the plain and take to the mountains."

Dias was silent for a minute. "I should say, señor, that first we had better journey down to Cuzco and then down to Sicuani, where the western Cordilleras, after making a bend, join the eastern branch, and there cross the Tinta volcano. On the other side are many gorges. In one of these I know there is some very rich gold sand. Explorers have sought for this spot in vain, but the secret has been well kept by the few who know it. It has been handed down in my father's family from father to son ever since the Spaniards came.

"I know generally several places where great treasure was hidden, but not the marks by which they could be discovered, and as we may be sure that every measure was taken to hide the entrances to the caves, the chances would be all against our lighting upon them. I may say, señor, that, great as was the treasure of the Incas, that of the Chimoos or Chincas, a powerful people who inhabited part of this country, was fully as large; and traditions say that most of the treasures hidden were not those of the Incas, but of the Chimoos, who buried them when their country was invaded by the Incas.

"This is certainly the case with most of the treasures hidden to the west of the mountains. It was so at Pachacamac; it was so at Truxillo, where the Spaniards found three million and a half dollars of gold; and it is known that this was but a small hoard, and that the great one, many times larger, has never been discovered. Probably the secret has long been lost; for if there are but few who know where the Incas buried their gold, it may well be believed that the exact locality of the Chimoo treasures, which were buried more than eight hundred years ago, is now unknown, and that nothing but vague traditions have been handed down."

"That one can quite understand," Harry agreed, "when we consider how many of the Chimoos must have fallen in the struggle with the Incas, and how more than half the population were swept away by the Spaniards, to say nothing of those who have died in the wars of the last thirty years. It seems strange, however, that the treasures in the temple of Pachacamac were left untouched by the Incas and allowed to accumulate afterwards."

"It was so generally regarded as the sacred city," Dias said, "that, powerful as they were, the Incas did not attempt to interfere with it, as to do so would certainly have stirred up a formidable insurrection of the natives throughout the whole of their territory; and instead, therefore, of taking possession of the temple and dedicating it to their own god, they allowed it to remain untouched and the worship of the old gods to be carried on there, contenting themselves with building a temple of their own to the Sun-god close at hand."

"Well, Bertie," Harry said when Dias had left the room, "I think we may congratulate ourselves. I really think there is a chance of the expedition turning out a success."

"It certainly looks like it," Bertie agreed. "For your sake I hope it will be so. As for me, I am quite content; what with Indians and brigands, wild beasts, alligators, and snakes, the journey is likely to be an exciting one."

CHAPTER V

A TROPICAL FOREST

It took them over three weeks to reach Cuzco. They were travelling across a plateau thickly dotted with villages and small towns, and everywhere richly cultivated.

The travellers had no difficulty whatever in purchasing food and forage on the way. They always slept in their tents now, and preferred Donna Maria's cooking to that which they could obtain in the small and generally dirty inns in the towns.

By the time they reached Cuzco, Bertie was able to converse in Spanish with some fluency. On the way he rode either beside Dias and his wife, or with José; in either case an animated conversation was kept up, sometimes on the stirring events of the war of independence and the subsequent struggles, sometimes about life in England, its ways and customs, concerning which neither Maria nor José had any knowledge whatever.

The old capital of the Incas lay at the end of a valley about two miles in length, and about a mile in width. To the north of the city rose an abrupt hill, crowned by the great citadel with its three lines of walls, the hill being divided from those forming the side of the valley by two deep ravines, in which flowed little streams that ran through the city. The appearance of the town was striking. There were numerous churches, its streets ran at right angles to each other, and the massive stone houses dated from the early Spanish days, though they were surmounted for the most part by modern brickwork additions. Where the great Temple of the Sun once stood, the church of Santo Domingo had been built, a portion of the splendid building of the old faith being incorporated in it.

"In crossing the passes we shall have the benefit of the old roads of the Incas," Harry told Bertie, "but once we leave these the difficulties will be enormous. Dias said that it might be better to dispose of our mules altogether and get trained llamas in their place, as these can climb over rocks where no mule could obtain a foothold. But then it would be necessary to take with us one or two natives accustomed to their ways, and this would not suit us at all. However, I do think that it would be worth while to take two or three of these animals with us. They can carry a hundred pounds apiece; but as we may be going over extraordinarily rough country, fifty pounds would be sufficient. The advantage would be that we could establish a sort of central camp at the farthest spot to which the mules could go, and then make exploring expeditions with the llamas to carry provisions and tools. The llamas are not bad eating, so that if we found no other use for them they would assist our commissariat."

"How far can they go in a day, Harry?"

"Ten or twelve miles, and you may be sure that that is as much as we can do when we are among the mountains."

"Then I should think they would be very useful. I suppose there will be no difficulty in buying them?"

"None at all. A good many are brought in for sale to the market every day. Of course it would be necessary to get strong animals accustomed to burdens."

Before starting there was another long consultation between Harry and Dias as to which course it would be better to adopt. The most-frequented pass through the mountains was that to Paucartambo, forty miles north-east from Cuzco, at the mouth of the pass that leads down into the plains. Between this town and the Carabaya range, a hundred and fifty miles to the south, was to be found the rich gold deposit to which Dias had referred. So far, however, as the traditions he had received informed him, it was situated near the slopes of the Tinta volcano, and between that and Ayapata. The direct road to this spot was extremely difficult, and he was of opinion that the journey could be more easily performed by going to Paucartambo and then skirting the foot of the mountains.

"You will find no difficulty in obtaining food as you go along," he said; "wild turkeys, pheasants, and other birds are to be met with in that district. Moreover, there are many plantations which have been deserted owing to the depredations of the Chincas, a tribe who live on the tributaries of the Pueros, or as it used to be called, Rio Madre de Dios. Here you will find fields of maize still growing, sugar-cane, cacao, and rice. One after another the estates have been abandoned; at some of them the whole of the people on the farms were massacred, and in all the danger was so great that the proprietors found it imposible to work them. The one drawback to that road is that we may fall in with the Chincas, in which case they will certainly attack us. However, they are widely scattered through the forests, and we may not fall in with them. On the other hand, the track by the Tinta mountain from Sicuani is extremely difficult and dangerous. We might lose several of our animals in traversing it, and should have to depend entirely on what we carried for food."

"Then by all means let us go the other way, Dias. Were we to lose some of our mules it would be impossible to replace them, and it would be useless to find gold if we could not carry it away."

Two days later they started, four llamas having been added to the caravan. Dias explained that it would not be necessary to take any natives to attend to these animals, as, once started, they would follow the mules without difficulty, especially if they were fed with them before starting. Three days' travelling brought them to the little town, which lay very high up in the hills. The cold here was bitter, and the party needed all their wraps, and were glad to get in motion as soon as it was light. Passing over a range of mountains above Paucartambo, where a thin layer of snow crunched under their feet, they began the tremendous descent into the plain. In a short time the morning mist cleared away. The road led through a tropical forest. It took them over three hours to reach the river Chirimayu, a descent of eleven thousand feet in the course of eight miles.

Here they halted by the side of a splendid waterfall.

At a word from Dias they all set to work to take the burdens off the animals. A place was cleared for the tents. When these had been erected José collected dried sticks. A fire was soon lighted, and Maria began to prepare breakfast.

"Is it unhealthy here, Dias?"

"Not here, señors; we are still many hundred feet above the plain. In the forest there it is unhealthy for whites, the trees grow so thickly that it is difficult to penetrate them, swamps and morasses lie in many places, and the air is thick and heavy. We shall not go down there until we need. When we must descend we shall find an abundance of maize, and fruits of all sorts. The savages kill the people they find on the estates, but do not destroy the crops or devastate the fields. They are wise enough to know that these are useful to them, and though they are too lazy to work themselves they appreciate the good things that others have planted."

"It is rather early to make a halt, Dias."

"We have work to do, señor. In the first place we must

find a spot where large trees stand on the bank of the torrent. Two or three of these must be felled so that they fall across it; then we shall have to chop off the branches, lay them flat side by side, and make a bridge over which to take animals. After breakfast we must set about this work, and it will be too late before we finish to think of going farther to-day."

"It is well that we bought four good axes and plenty of rope at Cuzco," Harry said.

"We shall want them very often, señor. Three large torrents come down between this and the Tinta volcano, besides many smaller ones. Some rise from the hills to the north of us. These fall into others, which eventually combine to make the Madre de Dios. So far as is known boats can descend the river to the Amazon without meeting any obstacle, from a point only a few miles from the head of the Pueros, which we shall presently cross. The fact that there are no cataracts during the whole course from the hills to the junction of the rivers, shows how perfectly flat the great plain is."

"And did either the Incas or the Spaniards ever conquer the Chincas and cultivate these splendid plains?"

"The Incas drove them back some distance, señor, and forced them to pay a tribute, but they never conquered them. Doubtless they cultivated the land for some leagues from the foot of the mountains, as did the Spaniards, and it was considered the most fertile part of the Montaña, as their possessions this side of the Cordilleras were called. The Spaniards tried to push farther, but met with such stout opposition by the savages that they were forced to desist."

All were ready when Maria announced breakfast. After the meal they sat smoking for half an hour, reluctant to commence the heavy work before them.

"We had better be moving, señor," Dias said as he rose

to his feet, "or we shall not get the bridge made before dark."

A hundred yards from the camp they found three large trees growing close to each other near the edge of the stream.

"Now, señor, I will take this tree. The next is not quite so large, will you take that? I will help you when I am finished with my own. Your brother and José can work by turns at the other."

It was hard work, for the trees were over two feet across near the foot. Dias had felled his before the others had cut half-way through, and he then lent his aid to Harry, who was streaming with perspiration. Before long his tree was nearly ready to fall. José climbed it with the end of a long rope, which he secured to an upper bough. Dias then took the other end of the rope, crossed the torrent by the tree he had felled, and when José had come down and Harry had given a few more cuts with the axe, he was able to guide the tree in its fall almost directly across the stream. Then he took Bertie's tree in hand. In ten minutes this was lying beside the others. It took three hours' more work to cut off the branches and to lay the trees side by side, which was done with the aid of one of the mules. The smaller logs were packed in between them to make a level road, and when this was done the workers went back to the little camp. The sun was already setting, and Donna Maria had the cooking-pots simmering over the fire.

"The meal is ready," Maria said, "and I think we had better eat it at once, for the sky looks as if we were going to have rain."

"And thunder too," Dias said. "You had better begin; José and I will picket the mules and hobble the llamas. If they were to make off, we should have a lot of trouble in the morning."

The aspect of the sky had indeed changed. Masses of cloud hung on the tops of the hills, and scud was flying overhead.

Maria placed one of the cooking-pots and two tin plates, knives, and forks beside Harry and his brother, with two flat cakes of ground maize.

"Sit down and have your food at once," Harry said to her. "The rain will be down in bucketfuls before many minutes."

They were soon joined by Dias and José, the latter bringing up a large can of water from the stream. They had just finished when large drops of rain began to patter on the ground.

"Never mind the things," Harry said as he leapt to his feet. "Crawl under shelter at once; it is no use getting a wetting."

All at once made for the tents; and they were but just in time, for the rain began to fall in torrents, and a peal of thunder crashed out overhead as they got under the canvas.

Soon a deep sound, which was certainly not thunder, rose from the woods. It was answered again and again from different directions.

"They must be either pumas or jaguars, which are always called here lions and tigers," Harry told his brother.

The storm continued, and each clap of thunder was succeeded by roars, snarls, and hissing, and with strange cries and shrieks. During a momentary lull Harry shouted:

"Is there any fear of these beasts attacking us or the mules, Dias?"

"No, señor, they are too frightened by the thunder and lightning to think of doing so."

"What are those cries we hear?"

"Those are monkeys, señor. They are frightened both by the storm and by the roaring of the lions and tigers."

In spite of the noises, Harry and his brother both dropped off to sleep before long, being thoroughly worn out by the day's work. They were awakened by Dias opening the front of their little tent.

"The sun is up, señors, and it is a fine morning after the storm. Maria has got coffee ready, baked some cakes, and fried some slices of meat."

"All right, Dias! we will be out directly. We will first run up the bank a short distance, and have a dip."

"You won't be able to swim, señor. The bed of the torrent is full, and no swimmer could breast the water."

"All right! we will be careful."

Throwing on their ponchos, they went down to the stream and ran along the bank.

"The water is coming down like a racehorse, Bert, but just ahead it has overflowed its banks. We can have a bath there safely, though it is not deep enough for swimming."

After ten minutes' absence they returned to the camp. As soon as breakfast was over, the tents were packed up and the mules and llamas laden. Dias had given them a feed all round an hour before. The course they should take had been already agreed upon; they must descend to the plain, for it would be next to impossible to cross the ravines on the mountain-side.

"Each stream coming down from the hills," Dias said, "must be followed nearly up to its source, but for the next seventy or eighty miles the search need not be so careful as it must be afterwards. The place cannot be far from Tinta, but somewhere this side of it. We need not hurry, for there are two months to spare."

"How do you mean, Dias?"

"On a day that answers to the 21st of March, Coyllur—that is a star—will rise at midnight in a cleft in a peak. It can be seen only in the valley in which the stream that contains the gold runs down. This is what my father taught me; therefore there must be mountains to the south-east, and this can only be where the Cordilleras run east, which is the case at Tinta."

"That is excellent as far as it goes, if we happen to be in the right valley at the time, Dias, but it would not help us in the slightest if we were in any other valley. And we should have to wait a year before trying in another place."

"Yes, señor, but there are marks on the rocks of a particular kind. There are marks on rocks in other valleys, so that these should not be distinguished by Spaniards searching for the place. I should know the marks when I saw them."

"Then in that case, Dias, the star would not be of much use to us."

"I know not how that might be, señor, but as these instructions have been handed down from the time when the Spaniards arrived, it must surely in some way be useful, but in what way I cannot say.

"When the Spaniards came, forty thousand of the Incas' people left Cuzco and the neighbouring towns, and journeyed away down the mountains and out to the west. Since then no reliable news concerning them has been heard, but rumours have from time to time come from that direction to the effect that there is a great and wealthy city there. I say not that if we failed here we should attempt to find it. The dangers from the savages would be too great. There would be great forests to traverse, many rivers to be crossed. We might travel for years without ever finding their city. When we got there, we might be seized and put to death, and if we were spared we might not be able to make off with the treasure. I mention it to show that gold may be found in many other places besides this valley we are seeking."

Crossing the stream, they made their way down through the forest. It was toilsome work, as they often had to clear a way with axes through the undergrowth and tangle of creepers.

For the next three weeks they continued their way. During this time five or six ravines were investigated as far as they could be ascended. Samples were frequently taken from sand and gravel and washed, but though particles of gold were frequently found, they were not in sufficient quantity to promise good results from washing.

They had no difficulty in obtaining sufficient food; turkeys and pheasants were occasionally shot; a tapir was once killed, and, as they had brought hooks and lines with them, fish were frequently caught in the streams. These were of small size, but very good eating. But, as Dias said, they could not hope to find larger species, except far out in the plains, where the rivers were deep and sluggish.

The work was hard, but they were now accustomed to it. They often had to go a considerable distance before they could find trees available for bridging the torrents, but, on the other hand, they sometimes came upon some of much smaller girth than those they had first tackled. The labour in getting these down was comparatively slight. Sometimes these stood a little way from the stream, but after they were felled two mules could easily drag them to the site of the bridge. When on the march, Harry and his brother carried their double-barrelled guns, each with one barrel charged with shot suitable for pheasants or other birds, the other with buck-shot. Dias carried a rifle. Very seldom did they mount their mules, the ground being so rough and broken, and the boughs of the trees so thick, that it was less trouble to walk at the heads of their animals than to ride.

CHAPTER VI

AN INDIAN ATTACK

ONE day, as they were journeying through the forest, at the foot of the slopes, José gave a sudden exclamation.

"What is it?" Dias asked.

"I saw a naked Indian standing in front of that tree; he has gone now."

"Are you sure, José?"

"Quite sure. He was standing perfectly still, looking at us, but when I called to you he must have slipped round the tree. I took my eyes off him for a moment; when I looked again he was gone."

"Then we are in for trouble," Dias said gravely. "Of course it was one of the Chincas. No doubt he was alone, but you may be sure that he has made off to tell his companions he has seen us. He will know exactly how many we are, and how many animals we have. It may be twenty-four hours, it may be three or four days, before he makes his appearance again; but it is certain that, sooner or later, we shall hear of him."

"What had we better do, Dias?"

"We shall probably come to another stream before nightfall, señor. This we will follow up until we get to some ravine bare of trees. There we can fight them; in the forest we should have no chance. They would lie in ambush for us, climb into the trees and hide among the foliage, and the first we should know of their presence would be a shower of arrows; and as they are excellent marksmen, we should be all riddled at the first volley."

It was evening before they arrived at a stream. Here

they made a short halt while they gave a double handful of grain to each of the animals, then they pushed on again until it was too dark to go farther.

"Will it be safe to light a fire, Dias?"

"Yes, that will make no difference. They are not likely to attack us at night. Savages seldom travel after dark, partly because they are afraid of demons, partly because they would be liable to be pounced upon by wild beasts. But I do not think there is any chance of their overtaking us until to-morrow. The man José saw may have had companions close at hand, but they will know that we are well armed, and will do nothing until they have gathered a large number and feel sure that they can overpower us. They will probably take up the track to-morrow at daylight; but we have made a long march, and can calculate that we shall find some defensible position before they overtake us. José and I will keep watch to-night."

The night passed without an alarm.

An hour before daylight Dias gave all the animals a good feed of corn, and as soon as it was light they again started. They were already some distance up the mountain, and after eight hours' travelling they arrived at a gorge that suited their purpose. For two hundred yards the rocks rose perpendicularly on each side of the stream, which was but some thirty feet wide. No rain had fallen for some days, and the water was shallow enough at the foot of the cliff for the mules to make their way among the fallen rocks, through which it rushed impetuously. At the upper end the cliffs widened out into a basin some fifty yards across.

"We cannot do better than halt here," Dias said. "In two or three hours we can form a strong breast-work on the rocks nearly out to the middle of the stream, where the current is too swift for anyone to make his way up against it."

Working hard till it was dark, they piled up rocks and stones till they formed a breast-work four feet high on both sides. Some twelve feet in the centre were open. They had chosen a spot where so many fallen rocks lay in the stream that it needed comparatively little labour to fill up the gaps between them.

"I thought wood-chopping bad enough," Bertie said as they threw themselves down on the ground after completing their labour, "but it is a joke to this. My back is fairly broken, my arms feel as if they were pulled out of the sockets, my hands are cut, I have nearly squeezed two nails off."

"It has been hard work," Harry agreed; "still, we have made ourselves fairly safe, and we will get the walls a couple of feet higher in the morning. We shall only want to add to them on the lower face in order to form a sort of parapet that will shelter us as we lie down to fire, so it won't be anything like such hard work. Then we will fill in the rocks behind with small stones and sand to lie down upon."

"They will never be able to fight their way up to it," Dias said.

"We need have no fear on that score. The question is, can they get down into this valley behind us, the rocks look very steep and in most places almost perpendicular."

"They are steep, señor, but trees grow on them in many places, and these savages are like monkeys. We shall have to examine them very carefully when we have finished the wall. It we find that it is possible for anyone to get down, we must go up to the next gorge and see if we can find a better position."

"I suppose you think we are safe for to-night, Dias?"

"I don't think they will try to come up through the stream. They have keen eyes, but it would be so dark down there that even a cat could not see. They will guess that we have stopped here, and will certainly want to find out our position before they attack. One or two may come up as scouts, and in that case they may attack at daybreak. Of course two of us will keep watch; we can change every three hours. I will take the first watch with your brother, and you and José can take the next."

"José had better sleep," Maria put in; "he watched all last night. My eyes are as good as his, and I will watch with Don Harry."

Accordingly, as soon as it became dark Dias went to the wall with Bertie. José, after a last look at the mules, wrapped himself up in a blanket and lay down.

"I think I had better turn in to the tent," Harry said; "we have had two days' hard work, and the building of that wall has pretty nearly finished me, so if I don't get two or three hours' sleep to-night I am afraid I shall not be a very useful sentinel."

Five minutes later he was sound asleep, and when his brother roused him he could hardly believe that it was time for him to go on duty.

"Dias is waiting there. Will you come down?" the latter said. "You were sleeping like a top; I had to pull at your leg three times before you woke."

"I am coming," Harry said as he crawled out.

He was joined by Donna Maria, and, taking both his shot-gun and rifle, went forward with her to the barricade.

"I have had a good sleep, Dias; we will watch for the next four hours. It is eleven o'clock now, so you will be able at three to take it on till daylight."

"I will send and call you again an hour before that," Dias said. "If they attack, as I expect they will as soon as the dawn breaks, we had better have our whole force ready to meet them.'

So saying Dias went off.

Talking occasionally in low tones, but keeping up a vigilant watch, they were altogether hidden from the view of anyone coming up the stream, for they exposed only their eyes at the top of their heads above the rough parapet. No attempt had been made to fill up the spaces between the stones, so that, except for the rounded shape, it would be next to impossible to make them out between the rough rocks of the crest. Harry had laid his double-barrelled gun on the parapet in front of him. He had loaded both barrels with buck-shot, feeling that in the darkness he was far more likely to do execution with that weapon than with a rifle.

They had been some two hours on watch when Donna Maria touched his arm significantly. He gazed earnestly but could see nothing. A minute later, however, a rock about fifteen yards away seemed to change its shape. Before, it had been pointed, but just on one side of the top there was now a bulge.

"Do you see them?" Maria whispered. "I can make out one above the rocks; the other is standing against the wall."

There was no movement for two or three minutes, and Harry had no doubt that they were examining the two black lines of stones between which the water was rushing.

"There are two others on this side, señor," Maria whispered.

The pause was broken by the sharp tap of two arrows striking on the stones a few inches below their heads.

"Well, you have begun it," Harry muttered.

He had already sighted his gun at the head half-hidden by the rock. He now pulled the trigger, and then, turning, he fired the other barrel, aiming along the side of the cañon where the two men seen by his companion must be standing. The head disappeared, and loud cries broke from the other side. The stillness that had reigned in the valley was broken by a chorus of shrieks and roars, and the air overhead thrilled with the sound of innumerable wings. Harry on firing had laid down the fowling-piece and snatched up his rifle.

"Do you see any others?"

"Two men have run away; the one against the rocks on the other side was wounded, for I saw him throw up his arms, and it was he who screamed. The man by him dropped where he stood; the one behind the rock is killed, I saw his body carried away in the white water."

Half a minute later Dias and Bertie came up.

"That was a good beginning," Dias said. "After such a lesson they will attempt nothing more to-night, and I doubt whether they will come down in the morning. They can get sight of the barricades from that bend a hundred yards down, and I don't think they will dare come up when they see how ready we are for them."

Harry and Maria continued their watch, but no longer with the same intentness as before. They were sure that Dias would not have lain down unless he felt perfectly certain that the Chincas would make no fresh move until the morning, and they chatted gaily until, at two o'clock, Dias came up and relieved them.

Harry slept soundly until he was called.

"The sky is just beginning to get light, señor."

He turned out at once. José was already feeding the mules.

"You had better come along with me, José, and bring that gun of yours with you. If the savages do attack, it will be well to make a forcible impression on them."

Greatly pleased with the permission, José took up the old musket he carried and accompanied Harry.

"What have you got in that gun, José?"

"The charge of buck-shot that you gave me the other day, señor."

"All right! but don't fire unless they get close. The shot will not carry far like a bullet; but if fired when they are close it is better than any bullet, for you might hit half a dozen of them at once."

José had been allowed to practise at their halting-places, and though he could not be called a good shot, he could shoot well enough to do good execution at thirty or forty yards.

"Everything quiet, Dias?"

"I have seen nothing moving since I came out."

Presently, as it became light, a figure showed itself at the turn of the ravine.

"Don't fire at him," Harry said; "it is better that they should think that our guns won't reach them. Besides, if the beggars will leave us alone, I have no wish to harm them."

In a minute or two the figure disappeared behind the bend and two or three others came out. "They think that our guns won't carry so far, or we should have shot the first man."

For a quarter of an hour there were frequent changes, until at least fifty men had taken a look at them.

"Now there will be a council," Harry said as the last disappeared. "They see what they have got before them, and I have no doubt they don't like it."

"I don't think they will try it, señor," Dias said. "At any rate they will not do so until they have tried every other means of getting at us."

Half an hour passed, and then Harry said, "I will stop here with my brother, Dias, and you and José had better examine the hillsides and ascertain whether there is any place where they can come down. You know a great deal better than I where active naked-footed men could

E

clamber down. They might be able to descend with ease at a place that would look quite impossible to me."

Without a word Dias shouldered his rifle and walked away, followed by José. He returned in two hours.

"There are several places where I am sure the savages could come down. Now, señors, breakfast is ready; I will leave José here, and we will go and talk matters over while we eat. The tents are only a hundred yards away, so that if José shouts, we can be back here long before the savages get up, for they could not come fast through that torrent."

"It seems to me," Harry said after they had finished the meal, "that if there are only one or two points by which they could climb down we could prevent their doing so by picking them off; but if there are more, and they really come on in earnest, we could not stop them."

"There are many more than that," Dias replied. "I made out certainly four points on the right-hand side and three on the left where I could make my way down; there are probably twice as many where they could descend."

"Then I should say that the first thing to do is to go up through the gorge above and see whether there is any place that could be better defended than this. If we find such a spot, of course we could move to it; if not, we shall have to settle whether to go up the gorge till we get to some place where the mules can climb out of it, or stay here and fight it out. By camping on the stream at a point where it could not be forded, and making a breast-work with the bales, stones, and so on, I think we could certainly beat off any attack by daylight, but I admit that we should have no chance if they should make a rush during the night."

"I will go at once," said Dias, "and examine the river higher up."

An hour later Harry saw a number of figures appear

against the sky-line on both sides. As they were clustered together, and would afford a far better mark than a single Indian, he took a steady aim at the party on the southern hill and fired. He had aimed above rather than below them, as, had the ball struck much below, they might not hear it, whereas, if it went over their heads, they would certainly do so. A couple of seconds after firing he saw a sudden movement among the savages, and a moment later not one was to be seen. Donna Maria, who was standing close by him watching them, clapped her hands. "Your ball must have gone close to them," she said, "but I don't think you hit anyone."

"I did not try to do so," he said. "I wanted the ball to go just over their heads, so that they should know that even at that distance they were not safe. I have no doubt that astonishment as much as fear made them bolt. They'll be very careful how far they come down the side of the hill after that. Now for the fellows on the other side."

But these too had disappeared, having evidently noticed the effect produced upon the others. After a pause heads appeared here and there at the edge of the crests. Evidently the lesson had impressed them with the necessity for precaution, as they no longer kept together, and they had apparently crawled up to continue their investigations. Beyond keeping a watch to see that none had attempted to descend the slope Harry did not interfere with them. At times he strolled to the breast-work, but no movement had been seen in that direction. In two hours Dias returned.

"The gorge above is a quarter of a mile through, and very difficult to pass. It is half-blocked with great rocks in two or three places, and there would be immense difficulties in getting the mules over. Beyond that it widens again, but the extent is not more than half what it is here. The walls are almost perpendicular, and I do not think that it would be possible to climb them at any point. Farther up there is another ravine. It is very narrow—not half so wide as this—and the stream rushes with great velocity along it. Two hundred yards from the entrance the rocks close in completely, and there is a fall of water sixty or seventy feet high."

"Well, that settles the point, Dias. We cannot get the animals out except by the way they came in. As for ourselves, we might climb up at some point in this ravine, but not in the others."

"That is so, señor," Dias said. "The outlook is a bad one—that is to say, we may now be unable to reach the gold river in time—but so long as we stay here we may be safe. We have plenty of provisions, we can catch fish in the stream, and no doubt shall find birds in the bushes at the lower part of the slopes. I doubt whether the natives will dare come down those precipices at night. If they try to descend by day, we can very well defend ourselves."

"The only question is, how long will it take to tire them out?"

"That I cannot tell we know so little of the Chincas that we have nothing to go upon. Some savages have patience enough to wait for any time to carry out their revenge or slay an enemy; others are fickle, and though they may be fierce in attack, soon tire of waiting, and are eager to return to their homes again. I cannot think that they will speedily leave. They have assembled, many of them perhaps from considerable distances; they have had two days' march up here, and have lost at least two of their comrades. I think they will certainly not leave until absolutely convinced that they cannot get at us, but whether they may come to that decision in two days or a month I cannot say."

Two night and days passed. The Indians were still on the hills, and once or twice men came down some distance, but a shot from Harry's rifle sent them speedily back again. The third night Bertie was on watch; he saw nothing, but suddenly there came three sharp taps. He discharged one barrel of his gun at random down the ravine, and then held himself ready to fire the other as soon as he saw anyone approaching. It was an anxious minute for him before the other three ran up.

"What is it, Bertie; have you seen anything?"

"No, but three arrows tapped against the wall, so I fired one barrel to call you up, and have been looking out for someone to take a shot at with the other; but I have not seen anyone, though, as you may imagine, I looked out sharply."

"It is probable that after the lesson they got the other night they did not come so near, and that they merely shot their arrows to see if we were still on guard. However, we may as well stay here for a bit to see if anything comes of it."

Nothing happened, however, and they returned to the tents. Next morning Bertie said to his brother:

"Look here, Harry, I have a plan."

"Well?"

"In the first place, how much powder can you spare?"

"There is that great powder-horn José drags about with him to charge his musket with. It will contain about a couple of pounds, I should say."

"That ought to do, I think. Do you think that burned wood would do for charcoal?"

"It depends on what purpose you want it for."

"I want it to prevent the powder from going off with a bang."

"Oh, well, I should think that burned wood ground to a powder would be just as good as charcoal. So you are thinking of rockets? Your two pounds of powder won't make many of them—not above two fair-sized ones, and the betting is they would not go up."

"No, I am not thinking of rockets, but of squibs and crackers. I know when I was at school I made a lot of these, and they worked very well. My idea is that if we could crawl up close to where the Indians are assembled, each carrying a dozen squibs and as many crackers, we could light a lot of the crackers first and chuck them among them, and then send the squibs whirling about over their heads, with a good bang at the end. You know how superstitious they are—they'd think it was some kind of magic. You know how superstitious they are—they'd think it was some kind of magic. It would set them off running, and they would never stop till they were back in their own forests."

"Well, I really do think that that is a fine idea—a splendid idea! The only drawback is, that in order to carry it out we should want a lot of strong cartridge-paper, and we have no paper except our note-books."

"I have thought of that, Harry, though it bothered me for a good long time. You see, the cases are only to hold the powder and to burn regularly as the powder does. At first I thought we might find some wood like elder and get the pith out, just as we used to do for pop-guns, but that unfortunately would not burn. We might, however, make them of linen."

"But we have no linen."

"No, but our leather bed-bags are lined with that coarse sort of stuff they cover mattresses with."

"Tick, you mean?"

"Yes, tick. Now, it struck me that this would do for the crackers. We should have to cut it in strips three or four times the width of the cracker. Then we could get Maria to make us some stiff paste; starch would be better, but of course we have none. Then, taking a strip of the cloth, we would turn over one side of it an inch from the edge to make a sort of trough, pour in the gunpowder, carefully paste all the rest of it and fold it over and over, and then, when it begins to dry, double it up and tie it with string. We should then only have to add touchpaper, which, of course, we could make out of anything, and put into the end fold. We could break up a few of the cartridges, soak them in wetted powder, and then cut them up into small pieces and stick them into the ends of the crackers. The squibs will be easier; we should only have to paste one side of the strips and roll them up so as to form suitable cases. When these are dry we should put a thimbleful of powder into each, and then fill them up with powder and charcoal. In order to make sure of a loud bang we could undo a piece of rope and wind the strands round each case for an inch and a half from the bottom. Of course, when we had ground down the burned wood we would mix it with powder and try one or two of the squibs, so as to find the proportions of charcoal to be used."

"You have evidently thought it all out well, and I think it does you no end of credit. The first thing, of course, will be to get some wood and char it. I should think that you would require at least two pounds of that to two pounds of powder; but you had better only to do a little at first—just enough to make an experiment. You know it will require ramming down well."

When Dias, who was on watch, returned he found Bertie at work burning pieces of wood and scraping off the charred surface. Harry explained the plan to him. As he had frequently seen fireworks at Lima, Dias quickly grasped the idea.

"It is splendid, señor; those things will frighten them far more than guns. They will think so many devils have got among them, and we will heighten the effect by discharging every piece that we can among them. In their confusion they will think it is the fireworks that are killing them."

At noon the next day Bertie with assistance had four squibs and two crackers ready for trial.

All, with the exception of José, who was on watch, gathered round. The first squib exploded with a bang, the second did the same, but with less violence, the third went off in an explosive spurt, the fourth burned as a squib should do, though a little fiercely, and gave a good bang at the end. The crackers were equally satisfactory.

"Now, Bertie," Harry said, "we will put all hands on to the business. Donna Maria shall make a good stock of paste, and cut the tick into strips for both widths. You shall make the cases for the squibs. Dias and I will take charge of the manufacture of charcoal."

They were soon at work. By night the cases were all made and drying, and were left near the fire so as to be ready for filling in the morning.

"We will start at nine o'clock tomorrow evening, Dias," said Harry.

They then discussed the arrangement for the attack. Each was to carry a glowing brand, and when he got there, was to sling his gun behind him and hold twelve squibs in one hand and the brand in the other. When they approached within throwing distance of the savages, they were to lay their guns down beside them, and then Harry was to put the end of his squibs against his brand, and hurl the whole of them among the Indians. A few seconds later Bertie was to do the same, while Harry fired one barrel of buck-shot. Bertie was to fire as Dias threw a dozen crackers, and then José was to throw his squibs. Then all were to throw squibs and crackers as far as they could go; and the other two barrels of buck-shot and José's musket were to be poured in. By this time they calculated the savages would be in full flight, and the three rifles could then be used.

Harry was to hand his rifle to Dias before the firing began, and he and Bertie were to slip fresh cartridges into these guns and recap them before sending off the last batch of their fireworks, so as to have them in readiness either to empty their contents into the flying Indians, or to cover their retreat should the fireworks fail to effect the panic they hoped for. Their pistols were also to be reserved until the Indians fled. Donna Maria was to stay by the water, and start at once on her way back if Dias shouted to her to do so.

CHAPTER VII

THE SIGNAL STAR

The next evening, as soon as it was dark and the meal eaten, the tents were struck, the baggage all rolled up and packed on the animals, and the fireworks divided. When everything was in readiness they went together and made a breach in the breast-work wide enough for the mules to pass. At nine o'clock four brands were taken from the fire and the party started. When within fifty yards of the lower end of the ravine José went forward, and, returning in a few minutes, reported that no savages were on guard. A fire was burning outside the mouth of the ravine, and from the reflection on the rock he believed that another fire was alight inside.

Keeping close to the rock wall, they went along in single file until within forty or fifty yards of the fire; then, going down on their hands and knees, they crawled up a slight rise, from the top of which they could see a hundred or more natives gathered round a fire. Laying the guns down to be ready for instant action, and keeping themselves concealed in the herbage, Harry took his bundle of squibs from his pocket. They were but lightly tied together; slipping off the string he applied the ends to the brand. There was a sudden roar of fire, and waving them once round his head he hurled them into the midst of the assembly. There was a yell of astonishment as the missiles flew hither and thither, exploding with loud reports. The last had not exploded when Bertie's handful flew among them; then came the parcel from Dias, and at the same moment Harry poured a barrel of buck-shot among them, followed by a volley of crackers, while almost simultaneously Harry threw his squibs and Bertie fired a volley of buck-shot. For a moment the savages were paralysed, then many of them threw themselves on their faces in terror of these fiery demons, while others started in headlong flight.

"Send them off as quick as you can!" Harry shouted, as he discharged his second barrel into the flying natives. Bertie followed suit, and then both paused to reload while Dias and José hurled their remaining fireworks. By this time the last of the natives had leapt up and fled. José's musket and the three rifles cracked out, and then the little party rose to their feet and joined in a wild "Hip, hip, hurrah!"

"You can come up, Maria; they have all gone!" Dias cried out; and Maria joined them a minute later. More than a score of natives lay dead or badly wounded round their fire.

"What are we to do with the wounded?" Bertie asked.

"We can only leave them were they are," Harry said. "Some of the savages may have wandered away, or not have come down from the hills, and will return here unaware of what has happened, or one or two of the boldest may venture back again to look after their comrades. At any rate, we can do nothing for them. Let us go back at once and bring down the mules. I suppose you will sit down by the stream, and wait till we come back, Maria?"

"Yes," she said, "there is nothing to be afraid of now; but you can leave me one of your pistols in case one of these savages may be shamming dead."

"José will wait with her," Dias said.

"You take my gun, José; it is loaded," Harry said. "If any of them should move and try to crawl away, don't fire at them; but if they look about and seem inclined to make mischief, shoot at once."

Coming down with the animals the three men carried torches in each hand. The mules reached the mouth of the torrent without accident, and the llamas were then lifted of the baggage mules which had carried them, and all were turned loose to graze on the rich grass near the edge of the river. José and Dias went to the fire in the ravine and returned laden with burning brands, and a fire was soon blazing near the water. Two of them kept watch by turns at the spot from which they had fired, lest any of the wounded Indians should, on recovering, try to avenge their loss by sending arrows down amongst the party. During the night four of the fallen Indians, after first looking round cautiously, crawled away, and the watchers could hear them running fast through the bushes till they were beyond the light of the fire.

At dawn a start was made. The river was crossed at the pool where José had swum over. Dias, on examination, found that the water, even in the deepest part, was not more than breast-high. Accordingly he returned; Maria, kneeling on one of his shoulders and one of Harry's, was carried across without being wetted. Then they joined the animals, which were grazing a short distance away, and set off without delay. Although they kept a sharp look-out they saw no more of the Indians. They ascended several more streams unobserved. Rough carvings on the face of several of the rocks led them to carry their excursions farther than usual, but beyond a few ounces of gold, washed from the stream, they found nothing.

"They must have been put here for some purpose," said Dias.

"I have been thinking it over, Dias, and I should not be surprised if, as you thought, they were done to deceive searchers. You told me there were some marks by which you would be directed in the gold valley; it is quite likely that other marks might have been placed in the valleys so that the real ones would not be particularly noticed."

"That is possible, señor; they would certainly do everything they could to prevent anyone not in the secret from knowing. The mark I have to look for first is a serpent. It is carved on a rock at the end of a valley."

"In that case the indication of the star would not be necessary, Dias."

"That may be, señor; but the valley may be a large one, and the hiding-place very difficult to find, so that even when the valley was known, it would need the guidance of the star to take us to the right place."

"That may be so, Dias, if it were a hidden treasure that we were looking for; but as, according to your account, it is simply an extraordinary rich deposit in the river, I hardly see why the guidance of the star should be necessary when once the valley was known."

"That I cannot tell you, señor; but I am sure that it must be difficult to find, for the Spaniards searched everywhere for gold, and although the records of most of their discoveries still exist, there is no mention of such a find, nor is there any word of it among the Indian traditions."

A week before the appointed date they found themselves in the neighbourhood where they felt sure the cleft must lie. Mount Tinta was twenty miles in front of them, and from that point a range of mountains trended off almost at right angles to that which they were following. One lofty peak some thirty miles to the south-east rose above another.

"I believe that that is the peak," Dias said.

The next day they halted at the mouth of another valley, and as they unloaded the mules, Harry exclaimed: "See, Dias, there is a cleft in that peak! From here it looks as if it were a mere thread, and as if some giant had struck a mighty sword-cut into it."

"That is right. Sure enough, señor, this must be the valley. Now, let us look about for the serpent."

The search did not take them long. An isolated rock rose a quarter of a mile from the mouth, and on this was a rude representation of a serpent. The next morning they explored the valley thoroughly to a point where, five miles higher, it ceased abruptly, the rocks closing in on either side, and the stream coming down in a perpendicular fall from a point some eighty feet above them. Going down the river, they washed the gravel again and again, but without obtaining even as much gold as they had found several times before.

"I cannot understand it," Harry said, as they sat down to their meal at dusk. "Your tradition says nothing about hidden treasure, and yet there does not seem to be gold in the stream."

"It may be higher up, señor. We must ascend the hills on each side of the valley, and come down upon the river higher up."

Harry was on watch that night, and at one o'clock he roused the others up. "See!" he exclaimed later on; "there is a bright star apparently about a foot above the peak. I should think that must be the star. No doubt that will rise in exact line behind the cleft on the 21st, that is four days from now; probably it can only be seen when we are exactly in the line with the cleft and the position of the gold. This cleft is very narrow—no doubt the result of an earthquake. It certain goes straight through, and very likely it is some hundred yards across, so that unless we are exactly in the line we shan't see it. As soon as it is dark on the 21st we will all go some distance up the valley, where it is only about four or five hundred yards across. We will station ourselves fifty yards apart across it, then one of us is sure to see the star through the cleft. We had each better take two sticks with us. Whoever sees the star will fix one in the ground and then go backwards for a hundred yards, keeping the star in sight, and plant the other; then the line between those two sticks ought to lead us to the spot."

Each night the star rose nearer to the cleft. "There is no doubt we shall see it in the proper position to-morrow night," Harry said on the 20th of the month. "That certainly is strong proof that the tradition handed down to you, Dias, is correct."

They employed the next day in again searching for some indication that might assist them, but in vain. Dias and José both asserted that the tiny rift in the rocky peak looked wider from the middle of the valley than at any other point, and even Harry and his brother admitted that it could scarcely be seen from the foot of the hills on either side, and therefore it was agreed that Dias, Harry, and José should take their places only some forty yards apart across the centre; Maria and Bertie going farther, near the sides of the hills. When midnight approached they took their stations. Suddenly, Harry, who was standing by the side of the rivulet, exclaimed, "I see it!" It was more than a minute later before Dias saw it, while it was three or four minutes before José spoke, by which time Harry had crossed the streamlet and fixed his second rod some distance on the other side. Dias and José did the same. Bertie did not catch sight of it for some time after José, and Maria did not see it at all. Then they went back to their camping place.

"It is curious that I should have seen it before either of you, when you were standing so close to me," Harry said. "It was lower than I expected, and it is evident that the cleft must continue much farther down than we thought, and that it must be extremely narrow at the bottom. It is certainly a splendid guide, and there can be no mistaking it. Unless I had been standing on the exact line, I should not have noticed the star till later, and the crack is so much wider towards the top that it could probably be seen on a line half a mile across. It will be strange if we cannot find the place in the morning."

None attempted to sleep, and as soon as it became light they took picks and shovels and started up the valley. Harry gave an exclamation of surprise as, standing behind the first stick, he looked towards the second. "The line goes to the middle of that waterfall," he said.

This was so; for the stream made two or three sharp bends between the spot where he had crossed it and the foot of the falls.

"'Tis strange!" Dias said; "we have examined that spot more than once. There are great stones and boulders at the foot of the fall, and a large deep pool. Can a treasure be buried in that? If so, it will be hard indeed to get it."

Harry did not reply; his face was white with excitement. He walked forward slowly till he reached the edge of the pool. It was some fifteen yards across, and the colour of the water showed that it was very deep.

"I will dive, Harry," Bertie said; "I have gone down more than once in five fathoms of water to pick up an egg that has been thrown overboard." He stripped and swam out to the middle of the pool and dived. He was down about a minute, and on coming up swam to the shore. "I could find no bottom, Harry," he panted. "I am sure I must have gone down seven fathoms."

"Thank you, Bertie," Harry said quietly. "Let us search now behind the fall."

There were some four or five feet clear between the

sheet of water and the rock. Looking upwards as they stood, the wall actually overhung them, and they could see the edge where the water poured over unbroken.

"There may be a cave here," Harry went on, " and it may be covered by those rocks piled up for the purpose."

They searched every foot of the rock within reach, but there were no signs of any man's handiwork. The rock was solid, thickly covered with dripping moss and ferns which had flourished in the mist and spray that rose from the foot of the fall. This they had ruthlessly scraped off with their picks. Silently they went out again at the end, and stood hopelessly looking at the fall. It was some time before Harry said, "We must move some of those stones now. Let us go at once and cut down some young trees, for we can do nothing with our hands alone, but must use levers."

In an hour the levers were ready. They chose the central spot behind the fall, and then set to work. Some of the rocks were dislodged without much difficulty, but to move others, it was necessary to first get out the smaller ones, on which they rested. So they toiled on, stopping for half an hour in the middle of the day for food, and then renewing their work. By evening they had made an opening four or five feet wide at the top, and six feet deep, close to the wall. It was now getting dark, and all were fagged and weary with their work, the light was fading and they were glad to return to camp.

The next morning, as soon as it was fairly daylight, they drank a cup of coffee and started again to work. Harry went first into the hole they had made, and, kneeling down, struck a match to enable him to see the rock more thoroughly. He gave a slight exclamation, then said: "Open your knife, Bertie, and come in here and strike another match. I want both my hands."

"I have a torch here, señor."

"That is best; then light it, Bertie."

There was just room at the bottom for Bertie to stand by the side of his brother, who was lying down.

"Hold the torches as low as you can, Bertie."

Harry picked away with the point of his knife for a minute or two and then sat up.

"That is the top of a cave," he said. "Do you see, this crack along here is a straight one. That, I fancy, was the top of the entrance to the cave. That stone under it has a rough face, but on the top and sides it is straight. It is fitted in with cement, or something of that sort, and is soft for some distance in, and then becomes quite hard. I can just see that there are two stones underneath, also regularly cut."

Dias examined the stones.

"There is no doubt that that is the entrance to a cave, señor," he said as he joined them; and the three went out beyond the fall, for the noise of the water was too great for them to converse without difficulty behind the veil of water. José stayed behind to examine.

"Well, Dias, we have found the place where the treasure is hidden, but I don't think that we are much nearer. Certainly we have not strength sufficient to clear away those fallen stones, and probably the cave is blocked by a wall several feet thick. No doubt it is a natural cave, and it seems to me probable that they altered the course of the stream above, so that it should fall directly over the entrance. I think before we talk further about it we will go up there and take a look at it. If we find that the course has been changed that will settle the matter."

It took them an hour to climb the hill and make their way down to the gorge through which the river ran. They examined it carefully.

"It must always have come along here," Dias said. "There is no other possible channel; but there are marks of tools on the rocks on each side of the fall, and the water goes over so regularly that I think the rock must have been cut away at the bottom."

Fifty yards further on, the gorge widened out suddenly, and they paused with an exclamation of astonishment. Before them was a wide valley, filled to the spot where they were standing with a placid sheet of water four or five hundred yards wide, and extending to another gorge fully a mile away. Bertie was the first to find his voice.

"Here's a go! Who would have thought of finding a lake up in the hills here?"

"I did not know there was one," Dias said. "I have never heard of it. But that is not strange, for no one who came up the valley would dream that there was anything beyond that fall."

Harry had sat down and thought for some minutes, looking over the lake without speaking.

"I am afraid, Dias," he said at last, "that your tradition was a true one after all, and that the gold lay in the bed of a stream in the valley we now see filled up."

"But it must have always been a lake, señor," Dias said after thinking for a minute, "and could not have been shallower, for there is no other escape than the waterfall."

"It may have had some other way out," Harry said.

Dias looked carefully round the side of the valley. "There is no break in the hills that I can see, señor."

"No; but my firm conviction is that the top of that cave that we found behind the fall is really the top of a natural cave through which the stream originally flowed. It is certainly remarkable that there should be a cave immediately behind that fall. I thought at first that the stream above might have been diverted to hide it, but the ravine is so narrow that that could not be possible.

"I think that the passage was probably closed by the old people when they were first threatened by the invasion of the Incas. No doubt they would choose a season when the stream was almost dry. They had an unlimited supply of labour. They would first partially block up the tunnel, perhaps for the first fifty yards in, leaving only a small passage for the water to run through. They might then close the farther end with sacks of sand, and having the other stones all cut, build it up behind the sacks, and then go on with the work till it was solid; then no doubt they would heap stones and boulders against the face of the wall. By the time the Incas had conquered the country the valley would be a lake many feet deep. When the valley became full the water began to pour through this gap, which perhaps happened to be immediately over the mouth of the tunnel, or it may have been altered by a few yards to suit."

"And that all means, Harry—?" Bertie asked.

"That all means that we have no more chance of getting at the gold than if it were lying in the deepest soundings in the Pacific."

Bertie sat down with a gasp.

"There is no way of getting that water out," Harry went on quietly, "except by either cutting a channel here as deep as the bottom of the lake, or by blasting the stone in the tunnel. The one would require years of work, with two or three hundred experienced miners, and ten times as many labourers. The other would need twenty or thirty miners, and a hundred or two labourers. There is possibly another way. I have no doubt that, with a thousand horse-power engine, the lake could be pumped dry in time; but to transport the plant for such an engine and its boiler across the mountains would be an enormous undertaking; and even where it here, and put up and going, the difficulty of supplying it with fuel would be enormous. Certainly one could not get up a company with capital enough to carry out any one of the schemes merely on the strength of an Indian tradition; and with the uncertainty, even if they believed the tradition, whether the amount of gold recovered would be sufficient to repay the cost incurred.

"Well, we may as well go down to dinner."

CHAPTER VIII

BRIGANDS

Not until he got to the camp did Harry look round. When he caught a glimpse of the guide's face he went up to him and held out his hand.

"You must not take it to heart, Dias; it has been unfortunate, but that cannot be helped. Of course we are disappointed, but we may have better luck next time."

"But I don't know, señor, with certainty of any other place. No one was ever trusted with more than one secret, so that if the Spanish tortures wrung it out of him two treasures would not be lost."

"We need not talk any more about this place, Dias. We will get back to Cuzco and make a fresh start from there."

"In that case, señor, there is no doubt as to the best route. There is a pass over the mountains just on the other side of Mount Tinta; it leads to the town of Ayapata, which lies somewhere at the foot of that peak. I have never been there, but I know its situation. It is a very steep pass, but as it is used for mule traffic it cannot be very bad. Once we have passed over it on to the plateau we shall not be more than seventy or eighty miles from Cuzco."

"That is quite satisfactory. We will set off tomorrow."

That evening there was a slight stir among the animals which had just lain down. José leapt up and walked towards them.

"There is something the matter, Dias," he cried; "the

llamas are standing up with their ears forward. They see or hear something."

"It may be pumas or jaguars," Dias said. "Take your gun, señor."

He picked up his rifle, and Harry and Bertie followed suit, and further armed themselves with their shot-guns.

"You had best come with us, Maria," her husband said. "There is no saying where the beasts may be. See! the mules are standing up now and pulling at their head-ropes. Let us go among them, señors, our presence will pacify them."

They all moved towards the mules, which were standing huddled together. Dias and José spoke to them and patted them.

"You stand at their heads, Maria," the former said, and keep on talking to them. We must see if we can discover the beasts. "There is one of them!" he exclaimed, but in a low tone. Do you see the two bright points of light? That is the reflection of the fire in his eyes."

"Shall I fire?"

"No, señor, not yet. If we were only to wound him he would charge us; let us wait till he gets closer. Probably there are two of them, male and female, they generally go about in pairs."

Even as he spoke the seeming sparks disappeared.

"He has moved," Dias said; "he will probably walk round us two or three times before he makes up his mind to attack."

Ten minutes passed and then Maria said:

"There are two of them. I can see their outlines distinctly."

A minute or two later there was a snarling growl.

"They are jaguars," Dias said.

Again and again the threatening sound was heard,

and in spite of Maria's efforts the mules were almost mad with fright.

"We had better lie down beyond them," Dias said. "There is no doubt the beasts will come from that side."

They lay down side by side on the grass with their rifles at their shoulders.

"I can see them now, Dias," Harry whispered, "not more than fifty yards away."

The beasts had now apparently made up their minds to attack. They crouched low, almost dragging their bellies on the ground, and one was somewhat in advance of the other.

"Aim between the eyes, Bertie, and fire when I do." Harry whispered to his brother, who was lying next to him.

When within twelve yards the leading jaguar halted.

"Now!" Harry said, and they discharged their rifles at the same moment, and, dropping them, grasped the shotguns.

The jaguar fell over on one side, clawing the air, and then rolled over and remained motionless.

Dias had fired at the same moment, but he had not stopped the jaguar. In another instant a dark body bounded over their heads on to the back of one of the mules, which it struck to the ground.

Harry and Bertie leapt to their feet, and discharged their second barrels into the jaguar's body. It turned suddenly round and attempted to spring, but its hind-quarters were paralysed; and Bertie, pulling out his pistol, fired both barrels into its head. The brute at once fell over dead.

"Thank goodness that is over without accident!" Harry said. "I am afraid we have lost a mule."

"I think not, señor. He was knocked down by the

shock, but he had his saddle on, and the brute had no time to carry him off: "

The mule rose to its feet as they spoke; José ran and brought a flaming brand from the fire. Blood was streaming from both the animal's shoulders.

"It stuck its claws in, señor, but has not made long gashes. The animal will be all right in a day or two."

Two days later they arrived at the foot of the pass. Just as they gained it they met two muleteers coming down it. Dias entered into conversation with them, while the others erected tents, preparing to camp.

"What is the news, Dias?" Harry asked as he returned.

"The men say, señor, that the pass is very unsafe. Many robberies have taken place in it, and several men, who endeavoured to defend themselves against the brigands, have been killed. They were questioned by four armed men as they came down, and the goods they were carrying down to Ayapata were taken from them. They say that traffic has almost ceased on the road."

"Is there no other way of crossing the mountains than by this pass?"

"There is a pass, señor, betwen Ayapata and Crucero, but it is a very bad one."

"And where should we be then, Dias?"

"Well, señor, it would take us along the other side of the mountains to Macari. From that place there is an easy path to La Raya; there we are on the plateau again, and have only to travel by the road through Sicuani to Cuzco."

"In fact, it would double the length of our journey to Cuzco?"

"Yes, señor."

By this time José had lit a fire, and they had seated themselves by it.

"One hates turning back, but we are not pressed for

time. As far as I can see, my only chance is the feeble one of finding treasure in the place you spoke of up the coast above Callao. It is now four months since we left Lima. Travelling straight to that place would take us how long?"

"Well, señor, if we go round by Ayapata to Crucero, and then to Macari, it would be nearly a thousand miles."

"Quite a thousand, I should think. That is three months' steady work. By the time we get there it will be about a year from the time we left England. I have seen quite enough of the mountains to know that our chance of finding anything among them is so small that it is not worth thinking of. It seems to me, therefore, Dias, that we might just as well return by the foot of the mountains as we have come, going through Paucartambo, crossing the rivers that flow north and fall somewhere or other into the Amazon, and keeping along it till we come to Cerro de Pasco. There we should be nearly in a line with this place you know of, and can keep due west—that is to say, as nearly due west as the mountains will allow. It would be three or four hundred miles shorter than by taking the pass at Ayapata. We should have a good deal of sport by the way, and should have no trouble with the brigands till we got to Cerro. What do you say to that?"

"It is certainly shorter, señor; and, as you say, we should have no trouble with the brigands, and we should also escape the troubles that have been going on for some years, and are likely, as far as anyone can see, to go on for ever. We were very fortunate in not meeting any of the armies that are always marching about."

Three months were spent in the journey to the foot of the pass leading up to Cerro. They had good shooting, and found no difficulty in providing themselves with food. Fish were plentiful in the streams, and in some of the long-deserted plantations they found bananas, grapes, and other fruits in abundance, together with sugar-canes, tomatoes, maize growing wild, and potatoes which were reverting to the wild type.

The next day's journey took them far up into the hills, and they camped that night at the upper end of a deep ravine. It had been a hard day's work, for at several points the mules had to be unloaded and taken up singly, and the loads then carried up. Fortunately, the packs were now very light, and were carried or hauled up without much difficulty.

In the morning they again started. They were just issuing from the ravine when a party of ten armed men made their appearance from amongst some rocks, and shouted to them to halt. Dias rode in front.

"You speak to them, Dias. Keep them for a minute in talk if you can, and then take shelter behind that boulder."

Then Harry ran back to José, who was walking with a leading mule twenty paces behind.

"Turn them back again, José. Halt a little way down, and then come up; there are some brigands ahead. Bertie, bring up your rifle and the two shot-guns. Tell Maria to remain with the mules."

Then he ran back again just as a shot rang out, and, dodging among the fallen rocks, he took shelter behind one abreast with Dias. "Was it you who fired?" he asked.

"No, one of the brigands. The ball went through the brim of my sombrero. I think they are talking to each other, they know there is no hurry."

"Hail them again, Dias, but don't show yourself above the rock."

"What do you want? Why did you fire at me?"

"We want everything you have got," a voice came back —"your mules and their burdens, and your arms. If you will give them up without resistance, we will let you up the pass without hindering you."

"Tell them that you must talk it over with the others, Dias."

"Well, we will give you five minutes," the man called back. "If you do not accept our terms, we will cut your throats."

Dias stood up, and walked quietly down the rugged pass. At the point where the mules stopped, the rock rose almost perpendicularly on each side.

"Maria," he said, "do you and José take off the saddles and bags and fill up the spaces between these rocks on each side. Get the animals in behind them. You stop with them, Maria. I have got five minutes, and will help you."

"You had better go up at once, señor," he went on to Bertie, "and help your brother, so that they may not get sight of you. However, I am afraid they know how many we are. It was foolish to light that fire yesterday evening. I expect they were somewhere near and caught sight of us, and no doubt one of them crept quietly down to find out what our force was."

Bertie had by this time got the guns unstrapped, and had filled his pockets with cartridges. He now went forward, and as he kept among the rocks he was able to get within four or five yards of his brother without being seen, as the mouth of the pass was almost blocked with great boulders.

"I cannot get any nearer without running the risk of being seen. I have loaded the double-barrelled guns."

"Stay where you are then, Bertie. I don't think they will make a rush, and if they do, you can use them as well as your rifle. Of course I have my pistols and you have yours."

"Now, then, the five minutes are up!" the brigand shouted.

"I am coming!" Dias shouted back.

As he approached, Harry said: "Stand by the side of a rock, Dias, so as to be able to shelter as soon as you have given them the answer; they are likely enough to fire a volley."

"We will give you nothing," Dias shouted. "Anything you want you had better come and take."

Three men raised their heads above the rocks and fired. Almost at the same instant Harry's rifle and Bertie's cracked out, the heads disappeared, and a fierce yell of rage showed that one, if not both of the shots had found their mark.

"Now, Dias, what do you think is our best move?"

"I don't know, señor. I fancy there are only eight of them now. At present I have no doubt they are talking, and I think we can safely get back to where we piled up the saddles and bales. We can defend ourselves better there than here. We can then talk matters over quietly."

"That will be the best plan, Dias, certainly."

Keeping under cover as well as they could they retired to the barricade, thirty yards lower. José, aided by Maria, had completed the defence. They had not, however, attempted to block the passage between the two great rocks. It was but three feet wide; the rocks lay about six feet from the cliffs on either side, and these spaces were partly filled by smaller fragments. Wherever there were open spaces the blankets had been thrust in from behind.

"Well done!" Harry said as they passed through the entrance.

"I told them not to close the path," Dias said. "We can do that now we are all together. Most of the rocks are too heavy for José and Maria to lift. Shall we build it up now, señor? I am sure they cannot force their way through while we four are holding the barricade."

"Certainly not, Dias, and I have no fear of their attempting it. But I think it would be as well for us to close it, otherwise we could not cross from one side to the other without exposing ourselves."

It took them two hours' hard work—the harder because the stones had to be thrown into the passage from the sides, as the brigands might be crouching among the rocks higher up waiting for an opportunity to get a shot. At the end of the two hours the gap was filled up to the height of six feet.

"Now we can talk matters over quietly, Dias," Harry said. "We may take it that, whether they attack by day or by night, we can beat them off. There is a little rill of water that trickles down along the centre, so we need not fear being driven out by thirst, and we have food enough to last us a fortnight. That is settled. Now are there any other passes near?"

"The nearest, señor, is on the other branch of the Palcazu—the river we followed till we entered the passes—and is about thirty miles to the north. The pass starts from a spot about fifteen miles above the junction, and goes up to Huaca, a place that is little more than ten miles south of Huanuco. From Huaca we could either follow the road to Cerro, or strike across the Western Cordilleras to Aguamiro."

"Then I think, Dias, that our best plan will be to go down again into the valley we left yesterday morning and then strike across for the mouth of this pass you speak of. You know the direction?"

"I know the general direction, although I have never been along there."

"Well, Dias, you must be the guide. I should say the sooner we start the better. My idea is this: If you with your wife and José will start at once, so as to be down the pass before it gets dark, my brother and I will remain here. You will leave our riding mules at the point where the track is good enough for us to gallop on."

"Why could we not all go together?" Maria asked.

"Because if there were no one here the brigands might discover that we had gone, within an hour or so of our starting. They might fire a shot or two, and, finding that we did not answer, crawl gradually down till they got here, for it must seem possible to them that we should return down the pass; and as there is no getting the baggage mules to go fast, we might very well be overtaken."

"But how are you to find your way, señor?" Dias said.

"We shall follow the valley down till we come to the spot where you have struck off. You can fasten a white handkerchief to a stick and put it in some bare place where we are sure to see it. I want you to halt when you get to the river somewhere opposite the mouth of the pass. We will ride nearly due north, and when we strike the river will follow it down till we reach you."

"We can't halt opposite the mouth of the pass, for the river there is already some size, and we could not cross it. I shall keep along near the foot of the hills—the water there is shallow enough to ford. Then I will follow it down until, as you say, near the entrance to the pass, and there stop on the bank till you come."

"That will do very well. In that case it won't matter much where we strike the stream, as our mules can swim across easily enough —they have had plenty of practice during the past six months. However, we will turn off north where we can see your signal."

"When will you leave, señor?"

"To-morrow morning. As soon as it gets dark we will light two torches and put them down at the foot of the barricade, so that we shall be in the shadow. These will show them that we are still here, and they won't care to venture down into the circle of light. We have let them know what a fomidable amount of firearms we have, and have given them a lesson that we can shoot straight."

"They certainly would not come, señor, as long as your torches are burning, but three hours are as much as you can reckon upon their burning."

"Well, we have a dozen left now, Dias, and when they burn out we must light two more and throw them over and trust to their burning as they lie among the stones. I shall manage to keep the lights going till daybreak, and shall start a good hour before that."

Half an hour later the party started, Dias having muffled the mules' hoofs, so that the clatter, as they passed over the rocks, might not be heard above.

The day passed slowly. The brothers took it by turns to keep watch, and just before dusk Harry said, "I think, Bertie, we might pull out the leaves and bush that Dias shoved into one of these gaps when he took the blankets and things out. I could push the torch through and fix it there, that would save having to cross the barricade. It is quite possible that one of those fellows may be keeping as sharp a look-out as we are doing, and it is as well not to set one's self up as a mark. If I put it through now it won't show much, while if I wait till darkness falls it will be an easy object to fire at. You keep a sharp look-out while I am doing this, and if you see either a head or a gun try to hit it."

Harry accomplished the operation without drawing a shot, and as soon as he had fixed the torch he again stopped the hole up behind it.

"It is evident that they are not watching us very closely," he said. "We will watch by turns tonight. It is six o'clock now; will you sit up till eleven, or shall I?"

"I don't care a bit. Which would you rather take?"

"I don't care;—however, I may as well take the first watch. We will start at five, so rouse me at four. If they come at all, which is possible, but not probable, it will be between four and five."

At ten o'clock Harry could see a glow of light at some distance from the mouth of the ravine, and in the stillness could occasionally catch the sound of voices. When he woke Bertie at twelve the lad looked at his watch and said, "You are an hour late in calling me, Harry."

"Yes, I had no inclination for sleep. The fellows have been reinforced. Of course I don't know to what extent, but I should say pretty strongly. They have lit a big fire some distance from the ravine. They would not have dared to light one if they had not felt themselves strong enough to fight us. No doubt they have half a dozen men on watch where we first saw them, and these would give notice if we were coming. I think we may as well fire a couple of shots, it will show them that we are here and on guard. They will suppose we thought we heard someone coming down to reconnoitre our position."

They both fired over the top of the barricade.

"I see you have renewed the torch, Harry," Bertie said as they reloaded.

"Yes, I have done so twice."

The torch was changed again at four o'clock, and a little later Bertie heard a slight noise.

"I think they are coming, Harry," he said quietly.

Harry was at once on his feet. "Use your rifle first, Bertie, and sling it over your shoulder before you give them the two barrels of buck-shot, so that you can start to run at once if we don't stop them."

"Yes, I am certain they are coming," he said, after listening for two or three minutes. "We have got two or three torches left, and I will give them the benefit of them."

He went back to the embers of the fire, lighted the torches, and, returning to the barrier threw them twenty or thirty yards up the ravine. There was a hoarse shout of anger, and then a dozen shots were fired. Bertie's rifle cracked out in return, and Harry's followed almost immediately. A dark group of some twenty or thirty men were rushing forward, and had just reached the line where the torches were burning, when four barrels of buck-shot were poured into them. Three or four fell, the rest fled at once, and the cries and oaths showed that many of them were wounded.

"They won't venture again for the present," Harry said. "You may be sure they will hold a council of war, so load again and then we will be off."

Two minutes later they were making their way carefully down the rocky passage, Harry carrying the bundle they had made up of the unconsumed provisions. As they had to exercise great care in climbing over the rocks, the day was just breaking when they came upon two mules that had been left behind for them. They rode cautiously until they were quite out of the ravine, and then started down the valley at a gallop. In an hour Bertie exclaimed, "There is the flag!" They rode to it and then turned off to the north, slackening their pace to a trot. At eleven o'clock they came upon the river. Here they waited for an hour, gave a couple of cakes to each animal, and ate the rest themselves. The river was some fifty yards across, but the mules only needed to swim about half this distance. The brothers kept beside them, placing one elbow on the saddles and holding their rifles and ammunition well above the water. They were soon across, and, mounting, followed the river down, letting the animals go their own pace, and sometimes walking beside them, as they wished to keep them fresh for the next day's work. At five in the afternoon they saw smoke ahead of them, and, riding faster now, soon joined their companions, who hailed their arrival with shouts of joy.

After the story had been told Dias said: "Well, there is no fear of our hearing any more of them. I expect you must have been gone hours before they found out that you had left."

"There is no chance of our being followed, I suppose, Dias?"

"Not the slightest. Being on foot, they have no chance of overtaking us, even if they could find the track."

The brothers were soon sound asleep, and did not wake till Dias called them, and said that Maria had coffee ready.

"What sort of a pass is it today, Dias?"

"Not a very bad one, señor. The one we tried yesterday hadn't been used for very many years, there is regular traffic up and down this; not valuable traffic, for Pozuco is a small place. They send up fruit and dried fish, and the oil they get from the fish; and bring back cloth, and such things as are required in the village."

"So there is nothing to tempt brigands to infest the pass and rob travellers?"

"No, señor. When I last went through it I heard no talk of them at all. They are more likely to infest the hills beyond Cerro, for near that place really valuable captures can be made."

The journey up the pass occupied two days. They met three or four small parties of men with donkeys or mules, but all these when questioned said that the pass was perfectly open, and that it was a very rare thing indeed for anyone to be robbed on the way. Late in the evening of the second day they arrived at Huaca. Two days later they started for Cerro, and arrived there forty-eight hours later after a rough journey through the hills.

"We never know in Peru, when we go to bed, who will be president when we wake," Dias said that evening. "There have been a dozen of them in the past five years, and altogether there has been trouble and civil war ever since the Spaniards left. I think that before we start it will be well that I at least should go on to Ayapata and find out what is doing. That would only delay us two days, and we might be better able to judge as to which route to take."

Accordingly next morning Dias went on ahead. On the following evening he rejoined them.

"There is fresh trouble in the south, señor. Colonel Vivancohidas has declared himself Regenerator of Peru, and is now marching against Gamarra, and General Castilla is advancing against him. The fighting will be somewhere near Arequipa. Whichever wins will presently cross the mountains and make for Cuzco."

CHAPTER IX

PRISONERS

WHEN they arrived at Cerro de Pasco they found that the division of Gamarra's army stationed in the district had mutinied and had declared for Vivancohidas, and were killing all those known as adherents of Gamarra. All traffic was at a stand-still. Numbers of the soldiers who did not choose to join in the mutiny had taken to the hills, and were pillaging convoys and peaceful travellers alike.

"I think, señor," Dias said, "that instead of crossing the Cordilleras to the west, as we had intended, it will be better for us to go south, skirt the lake of Junin, and make for Oroya. That is the route generally taken, for the passes west are terribly difficult. I have traversed this route many times, and when going with merchandise I always go through Oroya, though in returning from Cerro I take the shorter route."

"Very well, Dias, you are the best judge of that. It is a great nuisance that this rising should have taken place just as we want to traverse the country, but it can't be helped. I will go to the headquarters of Quinda—he is established at the mayor's house here—and get a pass from him."

The Peruvian colonel questioned Harry as to his motives for travelling there.

"I suppose," he said, "you have been searching for gold. We are sorely in need of funds, and I shall feel myself obliged to borrow any gold that you may have collected for the use of my army, giving you an order on the treasury at Lima, which will, of course, be honoured as soon as the authority of President Vivancohidas is established."

"I do not doubt the goodness of the security," Harry said quietly, "but while hunting I have not come upon any treasure. We have occasionally, when halting at streams, amused ourselves by doing a little gold-washing, but when I tell you that during the eight months since we started from Cuzco we have only collected about twenty ounces of gold, you may well suppose that no good fortune has attended us."

"Is that all, señor?"

"I give you my word of honour that is all, señor; and as I shall have to lay in a store of provisions and so on for my journey down to Lima, you may well imagine that it would be a serious inconvenience to me to part with it."

"Quite so, señor; so small a sum as that would not go far among the four thousand men under my command. However, I shall have pleasure in giving you the pass that you ask. You have had good sport, I hope?"

"As good as I expected. We kept ourselves in food, and have seen a splendid country, which I hope some time will again be cultivated, and add to the wealth of your country."

After a further exchange of compliments Harry returned to the inn where they had put up.

Next morning, after purchasing some coffee and other stores that were needed, they set out.

"Now we are all right, Dias," Harry said as they started.

"I hope so, señor; but from what I heard yesterday evening several strong bands of disaffected soldiers are in the hills between this and Oroya. Quinda's troops have by no means all joined him, and several companies that broke off have stationed themselves in the hills along this road. They have stopped and robbed more than one mule train with silver from the mines there. They have not meddled, as far as I hear, with Quinda's troops, but have simply seized the opportunity of perpetrating brigandage on a large scale."

"Well, we must take our chance, Dias. I hope we shan't fall in with any of those scoundrels."

"I hope not, señor. Perhaps we had better put our gold dust and money in José's boots. They are less likely to examine him than they are us. You had better put half in his boots, and give the other half to my wife to hide about her clothes."

They stopped for the night at a little village close to the lake. There was but one small room at the inn, but at the other end of the straggling village there was a yard where the mules could stand, and a loft where Dias, Maria, and José could sleep.

Harry and his brother had lain down but an hour on their blankets when there was shouting in the street, and two or three shots were fired. They leapt up.

"We had better hide our rifles and pistols," Harry said, "under that ragged bed that we did not care about sleeping on. We may possibly get them again even if we are robbed of everything else."

A minute later four or five men with a lantern rushed into the room. They were all armed with muskets, and one carried a torch.

"Who are you?" this man asked.

"We are English sportsmen," Harry said. "We have been shooting for some months at the foot of the hills, and are now returning to Lima. There are our guns, you see."

"We will take you before the captain," the man said. "Bring those guns along, Pedro and Juan."

The village was in an uproar. Some fifty men were occupied in searching the houses and in appropriating everything they thought useful. One house had been set on fire, and near this a man in an officer's uniform was standing. He heard the report of Harry's and Bertie's capture.

"English sportsmen, eh! How long have you been shooting?" he asked.

"Eight months."

"Eight months! Then guard them securely, Montes; they are doubtless rich Englishmen, and we shall get a good ransom for them. English señors who come out here to shoot must be men with plenty of money; but likely enough they are not sportsmen, but gold-seekers. However it matters little."

"I protest against this," Harry said. "Our consul at Lima will demand satisfaction from the government."

The other laughed.

"Government!" he said, "there is no government; and if there were, they would have no power up in the hills."

So saying he turned away.

Plunder that had been collected was brought in and divided among the party, four of the men with muskets keeping guard over the prisoners.

"I don't see anything of Dias and the mules," Bertie said in English.

"No, I have been expecting to see them brought up every minute. Now I am beginning to hope that they have got safely off. I think the fellows began their attack at our end of the village."

A quarter of an hour later the band started with their booty and prisoners for the hills. After a march of four hours they halted in a village in a valley running up into the hills. The prisoners were thrust into an empty hut, and four men with muskets told off as their guard. Next morning the captain of the band came in.

"I shall require a hundred thousand dollars for your ransom," he said.

"We could never pay such a sum," Harry said. "We are not rich men. I am a lieutenant on half-pay in the English navy, and, having nothing to do at home, came out with my brother for a year's sport. I could not pay a tenth of that sum."

"That we shall see," the man said. "If you cannot pay, your government can. You will at once write to your consul at Lima, telling him that if this hundred thousand dollars are not handed over to my messenger within four days of his arrival there, you will both have your throats cut."

"I will write the letter if you wish," Harry replied quietly, "but you won't get the money. If you like to say ten thousand dollars, I dare say the consul will do his best to raise that amount."

"One hundred thousand is the smallest sum," the man said angrily. "Write as I told you; here is paper, pen, and ink. Do not write in English. I will come back in a quarter of an hour for it."

"This is awkward, Bertie. It is evident that I must write. As to their paying twenty thousand pounds, the thing is absurd; if he had mentioned two thousand they might have considered the matter. Well, here goes!" and he wrote in Spanish the required message.

The robber on his return read it through.

"That will do," he said. "Now let me warn you, don't attempt to escape. You won't succeed if you do, and the sentries have orders to shoot you down should you attempt it."

The time passed slowly. The brigand was evidently determined to give them no chance of escaping and four sentries remained round the hut, one at each corner. In the daytime the prisoners were allowed to sit at the door of the hut, but they were shut up at nightfall. The guards were not allowed to speak to them, and there was therefore no chance of offering them a bribe.

On the fifth evening after their capture they saw approaching a peasant woman sitting on a mule. A man was walking beside her. Behind the woman was a small barrel, and two packs and two small wine-skins hung on each side.

"Harry," Bertie exclaimed, "I believe that is Dias and Maria!"

"It is," Harry said. "Thank God they have found us! Twenty to one they will get us out. What have they got with them, I wonder?"

They stopped in the road opposite the house, which was the end one in the village.

"You are not to come nearer," one of the sentries shouted.

"I am sure I don't want to come nearer," the woman said pertly. "You don't think you are so handsome that I want to get a better sight of your face?"

"What have you got there?" the man asked. "We shall be coming off duty in ten minutes."

"Well, we have got a little of everything," she said. "As pretty sashes as there are in the country, beautiful silk neckerchiefs, silver brooches for your sweethearts, and for those who purchase freely a glass of the best pisco spirit."

"Well, wait, and I dare say we shall lay out a dollar or two."

A minute or two later four other men sauntered up, and began to talk to Maria, who slipped off her mule. The guards, fearful that the best bargains would be sold before they could get forward, hurried the prisoners into the hut and bolted the door. The brothers heard a great deal of talking and arguing, and ten minutes later the sentries came up to their usual post.

"I would not mind betting odds," Bertie said with delight, "that Dias has drugged that spirit."

For a time the sentries talked, saying that the pedlars' goods were cheap and the spirit as good as any they had ever tasted. Gradually the talking ceased, and within an hour there was perfect quiet outside the hut. Half an hour later they heard footsteps coming quietly up to the door. They held their breath; but instead of, as they expected, hearing the bolt drawn, they heard the new-comers going round the hut, pausing a minute at each corner. Then they again stopped at the door; the two bolts were shot back, and the door opened.

"Come, señors," Dias said; "it is quite safe. We have put them all to sleep. Here are their muskets and pistols. You had better take them, in case we are pursued, which is not likely. At any rate, should one of them wake the want of a gun will mean delay in raising the alarm.

"Don't speak, señors; it is as well to keep quiet till we are fairly off." He shut the door and rebolted it, and then led the way down into the road.

Not a word was spoken till they had gone a hundred yards, and then Harry said: "You have done us another good turn, Dias; we did not see any possible way of getting out; but we both agreed that if you could find us you would."

"Of course, señors, you could not suppose that Maria and I would go quietly off."

"How did you manage to get away, Dias?"

"It was easy enough. After what we had heard of these brigands I made up my mind that I would not unsaddle the mules, nor take the packs off the two loaded ones. I told José to watch about half the night; but I was standing talking to him, and smoking my last cigarette, when he said suddenly, 'I can hear a noise at the other end of the village.'

"The evening was still, and I could also hear the sound of many footsteps, so I ran and pulled down the bar at the back of the yard, called Maria, and told her and José to take the mules straight down to the lake, and then to follow the bank. Then I ran to warn you; but before I got half-way I heard shouts and firing, and I knew that I was too late, so I ran back to the lake, where I overtook the mules, and we mounted and went off at a trot. When I got a quarter of a mile away I told the others to go on to Junin, which we knew was twenty miles away, and put up there till I joined them. Then I ran back to the village, and, keeping myself well behind a house, watched them getting ready to start, and saw you. There was nothing to do but to follow you. I did so, and observed where they had shut you up, and waited about for some hours, so as to see how you were guarded.

"I saw their captain, whose name is Valdez, go into your hut twice. When he came out a second time he had a paper in his hand. He went into the house he has taken possession of, and I kept a good watch over that. Presently two lieutenants came out, talking together. They entered another house, and ten minutes afterwards issued out again, dressed in ordinary clothes, such as a muleteer or a cultivator fairly well off would wear, and returned to the captain's house, and stayed there for a good half hour before they came out again. Two horses had been brought round to the door. The captain came out with them, and was evidently giving them some last instructions. Then they rode off, saying good-bye to some of the men as they passed through the village.

"Knowing the ways of these bandits, I had no doubt

the paper I saw their captain bring out of the hut where you were was a letter he had compelled you to write to request a large sum of money to be sent in exchange for you; and as I felt certain that we should rescue you somehow, I thought it was a pity that this letter should go down, so I started at once to follow them. They had not got more than a quarter of an hour's start of me, and by the line they had taken I saw that they intended to go to Junin.

"Fortunately I had some money in my pocket, and at the first farm I came to I bought a mule. It turned out to be a good animal, and I rode hard, for I wanted to get down to Junin before the two men. When I got to Junin I found Maria and José, who had put up the mules at the only inn there. I set Maria to watch on the road leading into the town, and went out with José to a little village a mile back, where I made sure the fellows would stop. I was not long in finding out that they had arrived about half an hour after after I had ridden through. That was good enough for me. We went back to the town. I had found that there was a road from the place where they had stopped, by which they could ride along by the lake without going into the town; so José and I ambushed there an hour before daylight, thinking that they would be off early. We were right; for in a quarter of an hour they came along. Day was just breaking, so we could make out their figures easily enough, and as they were not five yards away as they passed we were not likely to miss them. Well, I found the paper you had written in the coat-pocket of one of them, together with two hundred dollars, no doubt for the expenses of his journey. We hid the two bodies under a heap of stones."

"Then you killed them, Dias?" Harry said, in a tone of surprise.

"Of course! what else would one do with them? They were brigands, and they had attacked a peaceable village and killed several people. Even if I had not wanted to get your paper it would have been a very meritorious action."

"Oh, I am not blaming you, Dias, at all! There was no other way of getting the paper, and it may be regarded as an act of necessity. And what did you do with their horses?"

"José went on with them, and I returned to the town again and started with Maria and the mules. We journeyed to a village half way to Oroya. Of course we overtook José a mile or two after we had left Junin. There we put up at a quiet place and talked over the situation. Next morning Maria and I started back, bringing with us four mules, the fastest we had. We rode on two and led the others. I knew some people at Junin, for I have often passed through the town when I have been bringing down silver from Cerro, and one managed to get for us that little barrel of pisco. I was sure that no soldier would refuse a glass; but it was almost a sin to give such liquor to the dogs. Then we bought peasants' clothes, and a parcel of goods such as travelling hawkers carry.

"You know how we succeeded. Of course we had drugged the pisco heavily, and knew that two glasses would send any man off to sleep in half an hour. As soon as it was dark, Maria went on with the mule. We shall find her half a mile from here at a deserted hut where we left the other three mules."

"Well, Dias, you have assuredly saved our lives. Guarded as we were, there was not the slightest chance of our getting away by ourselves; and as the British consul certainly could not have raised the sum they demanded, we should have had our throats cut when the messengers returned empty-handed. Valdez is not the man to go back from his word in that respect."

"It is a pity you have lost your arms, señor."

"Yes, we have certainly lost our double-barrelled guns, but our rifles and pistols are hidden in the straw of the bed in the room where we slept. We had just time to hide them before the brigands burst into the room."

"Then we can recover them, señor. Of course I intended to ride straight to Junin, but it won't make very much difference. We will ride to the village, get the rifles and pistols, and then follow the road by the lake. It is now only nine o'clock; we can be there by one easily, and reach Junin by morning. It will be perfectly safe to rest there. I suppose your guards will be relieved about twelve o'clock?"

"Yes, that was the time we heard them changed."

"They will most likely discover that you have gone then. When they find the four guards sound asleep, they are sure to unbolt the door and see if you are there, then of course they will give the alarm at once. But I hardly think they will even attempt to pursue. They are infantry, and none of them are mounted but the officers, which means that at present only Valdez himself has a horse. They would know that you had been assisted, and that probably horses were waiting for you somewhere. There is the hut, señors."

Maria ran out as they came up.

"The saints be praised," she exclaimed, "that you are with us again, senors!"

"The saints are no doubt to be praised," Harry said, "but we feel at present a good deal more indebted to Dias and yourself than to them."

"We had better be moving at once," Dias said. "We are going down to the village where they were captured,

Maria. They hid their rifles and pistols there when they found the place in the hands of the brigands."

Three minutes later they started. There was a full moon, so they were able to ride fast, and it was just midnight when they arrived at the village. When they knocked at the house where their rifles had been left, the proprietor looked out from the upper window in great dismay, fearing that the brigands might have returned. However, as soon as he recognised the party he came down and opened the door. The arms were found were they had been hidden, and in five minutes they were again on their way, and arrived at Junin at five o'clock. It was necessary to wait here twenty-four hours to rest the animals. The next morning they started as soon as it was light, and picked up José and the convoy. The brothers mounted the two horses, and Dias and Maria rode on one mule, and led three behind them. Jose rode another and led four. The horses and the mule Dias had bought were sold at Oroya, and after purchasing enough provisions for the rest of their journey they started for Lima, having concluded that it would be better, now that they were on the main track, to follow it instead of striking across the hills.

CHAPTER X

THE CASTLE OF THE DEMONS

THE travellers met with no more trouble, and a fortnight later they rode into Lima and took up their quarters at the hotel. Dias asked that he might go on with the mules to his home.

"We want to know how things have gone on in our absence," he said. "I shall come in each day to see if you have any orders for mc."

"There will be no occasion for that, Dias. We have quite made up our minds to wait here for a week before starting our next expedition, so if you will come over in four days that will be quite soon enough."

As soon as Dias had gone on with the mules Harry went to the British consul's and found three letters waiting there for him, two from Miss Fortescue and one from Mr. Barnett. They were all full of encouragement, especially the former. He told his brother of their contents.

"Hilda says that if I don't succeed here, she will give herself, or rather her father, two years, and at the end of that time, if she doesn't find someone she likes better, she will marry me, whether he likes it or not—at least, that is what it comes to."

"I congratulate you, old boy. At the same time, it is evident that she would not have been worth her salt if she had arrived at any other conclusion."

To Harry's surprise the muleteer came in at ten o'clock next morning.

"Well, Dias, I did not expect to see you again so soon.

You have found everything right at home, I hope?"

"No, señor, I am sorry to say I did not. Three days after we left here our house was burnt down."

"Burnt down, Dias! How did it happen?"

"Everyone says that it must have been fired on purpose, for the flames seem to have burst out in all parts at once. No one in the town thought that I had an enemy in the world, and all have been wondering who could have had a grudge against me. Of course we need not go very far to guess who was at the bottom of it."

"I suppose not, Dias. It must have been those scoundrels we gave a thrashing to."

"There is no doubt of that, señor. But this time they have got the best of me, for they know very well that I have no proof against them, and that it would be useless to lodge any complaint."

"I am afraid it would, Dias. Is it quite burnt down?"

"The walls are standing señor. It takes a good deal to burn adobe."

"What do you suppose it would cost to put it in the same condition as before, with the furniture and everything?"

"No great thing, señor; two hundred or two hundred and fifty dollars. It would not be as much as that if it hadn't been that Maria had left her festa dresses and her silver trinkets behind. There was not much furniture in the house; but I think I could replace everything for about two hundred dollars, and I have a good deal more than that laid by."

"I shall certainly make that up to you, Dias. It was entirely your kindness in deciding to take us on Mr. Barnett's recommendation, and to undertake this journey, that brought the ill-will of these scoundrels upon you. Of course it is of no use doing anything now, but when our search is over I shall certainly see that you are not in any way the loser."

"No, señor; if I could not replace it myself I might accept your kind offer, but I can do it without breaking very heavily into my savings. And indeed their attack on me was the outcome of an old grudge."

"Well, do you think these fellows will try to play you another trick, Dias?"

"I hope they will," Dias said savagely, "that is, if they don't have too much odds against me. I owe them a big score now, for twice they have got the better of me. I should like to get even with them. But I hope, señors, that while you stop here you will never go out without your pistols. It is against you they have a grudge now more than me; it was owing to you that they failed in killing me."

"We will do so; and we won't carry sticks this time, so that if they see us going along they will think we are unarmed."

Whenever they went out after dark, indeed, Harry and Bertie had an idea that they were followed, and on their way home each invariably carried a cocked pistol in his pocket ready for instant use. It was as well that they did so, for on returning late one evening from señor Pasquez, four men suddenly sprang out upon them.

They were on their guard, and their arms went up in an instant, and two shots were fired. As the pistols were almost touching the men's heads when the trigger was pulled, both the assailants dropped dead, and the others at once took to their heels.

"There are two of Dias's enemies wiped out," Harry said quietly. "I hope the others will give us a chance before we leave. Well, let us walk on before the watch comes along. It would ruin our plans altogether if we were kept here for an indefinite time while enquiries are being made."

The next morning they heard from their waiter at breakfast that two men had been found dead in the street.

"They are muleteers," he said, "but are known to be bad characters, and are suspected of having been concerned in several murders. It is evident that they made a mistake this time, and have got what they deserved. They are known to be associated with others. There were five of them; one was killed in a knife fight some months ago, and a search has been made for the others, but it is not likely that they will be caught. They were probably concerned in the affair, and knowing that they would be suspected of having had a hand in this, and that their character will go against them, I expect they went off at once to the foot of the hills, and won't be heard of again for some time to come."

"I think it a pity they were not all shot. It is a shame that in a town like this people cannot walk in the streets after dark without the risk of being assassinated."

Dias was very pleased when, on coming up that morning he heard of what had happened. He quite agreed that the other men would almost certainly have taken to the mountains.

"Even if they have not, señor, you are safe from another attack. Now they know that you carry pistols, and are prepared for them, they will let you alone."

"When we come back here, Dias, we will give you a brace of our pistols, and I trust you will carry them in your pocket ready for use after dark, whether you are in Lima or at Miraflores."

"Thank you señor. I do not think they are likely to show their faces here again for a long time; but at any rate I will be on my guard, and will gratefully accept your offer of the pistols. Now, señors, I must set to work today to get in our stores for the next journey. I have made a list of what we shall want."

"Well I have plenty of money, Dias, for I find two remittances from home awaiting me here. We have already bought two double-barrelled guns and a stock of ammunition, principally buck-shot, for we shall not be doing much big game shooting. We can always buy food at the sea-side villages."

Three days later all was in readiness. The mules were brought up from Miraflores by José, accompanied by Maria, and an early start was made on the following morning.

"To-morrow, señor," Dias said, "you will see the spot I was telling you about, where, as the traditions say, the spirits of our ancestors inhabit the ruins of a building so old, that it was ancient when the Incas first came here. They are still there, and men who have been rash enough to approach the spot have been found torn to pieces as if by wild beasts; but none go near now."

"Did the Spaniards never go there?"

"I know not, sir; but 'tis likely they never even heard of it. The country is all dry and barren, and there were no mines to tempt them. The Indians never speak of it; those who were alive when the Spaniards came had some reason for not doing so; and even now you could go to the nearest village, which lies more than twenty miles away, and ask the people about it, but they would only say that they had never heard of it, that no such place existed, for they believe that even to speak of it would bring dire disaster. We Indians are Christians; the Spaniards made us so. We make the sign of the cross, and we bow before their images and pictures, and once a year we go to their churches; but among the tribes east of the mountains that is all. We believe in the traditions of our fathers and in the demons of the forest; and though on this side of the hills, where the Spaniards held a tight grip upon us, the people have well-nigh forgotten their old faith, they still believe in many of the tales they have learned from their fathers, and this of the Castle of the Demons, as it is called, is as strong as ever in these parts."

"Have you ever seen the castle, Dias?"

"I have seen it, señor. There is only one point from which it is visible. We shall go there tomorrow, it is ten miles from here. The castle lies in a rift of the rock. I should say that in ancient times this opened to the sea, but the building closed the entrance. Whatever it may have been, it does not rise above the summit of the cliff, which goes down as straight as a wall for miles on the sea face. The rift on the land side of the castle seems to have a width of about fifty feet, and I could see openings which were, I suppose, windows. The rocks on each side are higher than the castle itself, so that anyone coming along would not see it until he looked down upon it."

"But of course it is visible from the sea, Dias?"

"It would have been visible in the old days without a doubt, señor, but it cannot be seen now. The stones are the colour of the rocks beside them. They are stained and broken, and unless a boat went along within a very short distance none would dream that there was a break in the cliff there. I heard that from a fisherman whose boat was driven in by a gale and well-nigh lost. He said that he could see that the stones, which are very large—much larger than any of those in the remains of the buildings of the Incas—were not in regular lines."

"It is very strange that anyone should have taken the trouble to build a place in such a singular position. Is there not any legend as to its construction?"

"There is a tradition, señor, that it was built as a prison by the king of those times, a thousand years before the Spaniards came, and even before the people whom the Incas conquered came into the land, and that it was a place of imprisonment, some say of a wife, others of a son, who had rebelled against him. Some say that it was built by the demons, but as it happened long before our people came here, none can know."

"Well, Dias, it seems to me that this old place is very likely to have been used as a hiding place for treasure. As to these tales about demons, of course they are ridiculous. I took your advice when we were being opposed by fierce Indians, but when it is a question of demons, I can trust to my revolvers and rifles against a legion of them."

"Well, señor, you are the master. I have led you here as I promised. There may be treasure here or there may not. If you will go, you must; but I pray you not to command me to go with you. I would have followed you to the death through the swamps and forests on the other side, but I dare not risk being torn to death by demons and being left without burial. I will lead you to within two miles of it, and will wait three days for your return. If you come not then, I will return to my place and mourn for you."

"Very well, Dias, you may count upon my return long before three days are up. Now, in the first place, take me to the point from which I can have a view of the castle."

"We have had a long journey today, señor, and it is two hours' journey from here. We had better rest and go in the morning."

Harry nodded.

"We will be off early. You say it is ten miles from the spot where we shall see it. If we start at daybreak I can be there before noon, which will give me plenty of time for a first look round the place. We have got some torches left. I shall want them, for possibly there may be some chambers underground into which we shall have to penetrate."

"I will help you look, señor, and will work there as long as you like in the search, if you return and tell me that you have seen and heard nothing of the demons that are said to be there. I am not afraid of danger when I know that it is men that we have to do with. But I dread being strangled and torn, as the legends say that all who have ventured here have been."

Harry said no more.

"There, señor," Dias said, when at eight o'clock in the morning they stopped on a projecting spur of the hill, "that is the castle!"

From where they stood they could see that the ground fell away into what was at first a mere depression, but gradually deepened into a valley half a mile wide. Still farther down the sides became more precipitous, and in the distance the valley was closed in by rock walls, and appeared to come to an end. That it did not do so was evident from a streak of bright green in the centre of the valley, showing that a small stream must run down it. From the point at which they stood they could see the level line of the plateau near the cliff facing the sea, and on the surface of this a dark zigzag line marked the course of the ravine. Then, when apparently close to the termination of the flat land by the cliffs, the dark streak widened out somewhat. Through a small but powerful telescope which Harry carried he could make out distinctly the upper part of what might be a house.

"It is a strange-looking place for a castle to be built," he said, "but it quite answers to your description, Dias. There are certainly some openings, which may have been windows. I am sure no one looking from here, and ignorant that such a place existed, would notice it, and of course from the valley it could not be seen at all. Even from this height I do not think I can see more than ten or twelve feet of the upper part. But surely it must be noticeable to anyone coming along the cliffs?"

"It may be, señor, but I cannot say. Certainly no native would go along there in the daytime. Still, it does seem likely that in the Spanish time some one must have ridden along the top of the cliffs, and if they had seen the castle it would certainly have been searched. Assuredly it has not been so. I have been at Ancon and Salinas many times, and have talked with the people there. They would never speak on the subject to one of white blood, but knowing that I was of native blood, and belonged to one of the families to whom the secret could be strictly trusted, they were ready enough to talk about the Castle of Demons. Had the Spaniards ever searched it they would have known, and the place would no longer be feared; but all say that from the time of the conquest by the Spaniards no living being has, as far as is known, entered it."

"Then the Incas knew of it, Dias?"

"I think so, señor, though I have not heard that any of them ever lived there; but tradition says that the vessel in which a great store of treasure was sent away from Pachacamac, and which, as is proved by Spanish writings, was never heard of afterwards, and doubtless was sunk in a great storm that came on two or three days after it sailed, was intended to be landed and hidden in this castle, which they thought might well escape the observation of the Spaniards."

"And even among your traditions there is no allusion to what became of this treasure ship?"

"No, señor; all traditions say that it was never heard of from the day it sailed. Had it landed at that castle the secret would have been handed down to some of the native families, just as that of the golden valley and of other hidden treasures has been. But there can be no doubt that the ship was lost with all her treasure."

They stopped half an hour for breakfast and then rode down the valley. When they got near the spot where it closed in Harry saw by the pallor on the native's face that he was beginning to be greatly alarmed.

"You had better stop here, Dias. My brother and I will go on and explore this ravine and have a look at the place. We will take some ropes with us, for the ravine may be blocked by falls of rocks, and we may have to let ourselves down. Evidently the water gets to the sea, or this valley would be a lake like that in the golden ravine, for although it is but a mere driblet of water now, you can see by the banks that a considerable amount comes down in the wet season. How it gets past the castle I don't know; I can only suppose that there is a passage for it underneath the building. We will take both our guns, Bertie, and our pistols. There are no demons we are quite sure, but the place may have been used as a hiding-place for outlaws and brigands, who could find no better spot, as there was no fear whatever of its being discovered. We will take some bread and meat in our haversacks and a flask of spirits. Perhaps we shall be away longer than we expect, Dias, but at any rate we will not stop there after dark."

Tears were in the Indian's eyes as Harry and Bertie said good-bye to him.

"There is no humbug about Dias," Bertie said as they left the others. "He is really in a blue funk."

"Yes, he is quite in earnest; and we know that he is no coward in other matters."

"Certainly not. He showed any amount of pluck in the affair with the Indians. But he seems such a bright, sensible sort of chap, that it is quite funny to hear him going on about his demons. I should not be surprised at anything the ordinary peasant might believe, but it is different with a man like Dias."

"You know, Bertie," Harry said, coming to a sudden stop, "I think we are making a mistake going on into this ravine. I have no belief that the place is inhabited; still, there may be desperadoes, and perhaps a few fanatics. It is not more than a mile at the outside to the place where we can climb the hillside. In that way we shall be able to look down into this ravine, and take a general view of the place. We shall know what we are doing then, whereas if we were to go on through the gorge without knowing anything about it, we might find ourselves caught in a trap. It won't make half an hour's difference for the ground up there will be as good walking as it is here, while we might find all sorts of obstacles in this ravine, and with two guns apiece, ammunition, pistols, coils of rope, food, and so on, we should find it awkward work climbing among heaps of rocks."

On gaining the plateau they followed the crest of the valley until they came to a spot where the ravine appeared to end. They found that in fact it made a sharp turn. It was here only some ten feet wide, but soon broadened out to thirty. Fifty yards farther there was another sharp bend, the ravine narrowed to twenty feet, and the sides became absolutely perpendicular. Twenty yards farther still they saw something like a wall about thirty or forty feet high stretching across the gorge, which was here some seventy feet deep. About twenty feet from the foot there was a steep ascent of rocks, such as might have fallen there by a slip from one side or the other. Above these a perpendicular wall rose for another twenty-five feet. Harry and his brother looked at it in surprise from the height at which they stood. Its appearance was precisely that of the wall-precipices on each side. It was rough and uneven, and they could see no signs of any joints.

"It looks as if it were natural," Bertie said, "but it can't be."

"No, it must certainly be artificial, but it is wonderful imitation, and certainly anyone coming up the ravine would suppose that bank of rocks at the foot had fallen from its face; but we know that it can't be that, for the water makes its way through. Besides, you see it is only three feet wide at the top, and then there is a narrow ledge a couple of feet wide, which was evidently made for the garrison to stand upon and shoot their arrows at anyone attempting to come up the ravine. Behind the slope is all rough rocks, except just below our feet, where there is a narrow stone staircase of regularly-cut steps. It is so narrow that it could not be noticed by anyone standing here, unless they bent over to look straight down as I am doing. Well, it is just as well that we made the circuit, for we certainly could not have climbed over there."

Another sharp turn, and the ravine ran straight towards the castle. They hurried on, and when they had gone fifty yards stood at the edge of a roughly circular pit. It was seventy or eighty feet across, narrowing at each end. At one end was the ravine at whose mouth they were standing, and directly opposite, in what might be called the neck of the bottle, stood the Castle of the Demons. It was some fifty feet in width, and as it stood back about forty feet up the neck it could hardly be seen at any point except that at which they were standing. There was no door or other opening at less than some twenty-five feet from the ground. At that height was a broad aperture about four feet high and twelve wide. Above this were several smaller openings about four feet square. The singular point in the structure was a rough arch of rock, which extended above it and formed its roof. This arch projected thirty or forty feet in front of the building, so that the latter had the appearance of standing in a great cave.

"What an extraordinary-looking place!" Bertie said in a low voice.

"Extraordinary, but how splendidly chosen for concealment! You see the top of the rock above it is level with the ground on either side. This would perfectly well account for people riding along the line of the cliffs, and passing over without dreaming that there was a house below them. Even if they went to the edge on this side, they would simply see this deep pit and the ravine beyond, but could not by any possibility obtain a sight of the house unless they came round to nearly where we are standing, which they could have no possible motive for doing. Besides, you see, all the way we have been passing through a thick bush; and I have no doubt that in the old time a wood stood here, possibly planted by the builders of the house. Of course the arch existed before the house was built. The stratum below was probably softer, and the stream gradually trickled through, and perhaps in some great flood, when this basin was full, burst its way out, after which the rock gradually fell until it formed that great natural arch."

"Well let us go round and have a look at the other side."

They found that the width of the arch to the sea cliff was a hundred and fifty feet.

"If the castle extends to this face, Bertie, it is a hundred feet across, but from here we can't see whether it does so. It is probably built flush, however, as Dias said that it was not noticeable from the sea, and had the arch projected beyond it it could certainly have been seen."

"Well, Harry, if you will tie a rope round my waist you can let me down, and I will have a look at it."

"All right, Bertie."

Bertie laid down his weapons and water-flask, made a loop at the end of one of the ropes they had brought large enough for him to sit in, then he looked for a spot where the grass extended to the very edge. "This is a good place, and the rope won't chafe as it runs over that. Now I am ready. If you will go back to that tree-stump fifteen feet away and let it out gradually, I will be off."

He knelt down, and putting the rope over his head took a firm hold of it just above the loop, and then crawled backwards, his brother keeping the rope taut. "Slack it out gradually now," Bertie said; "I am just over."

Directly afterwards his shoulders disappeared. Harry let the rope slowly out until he calculated that fifty feet were over the cliff, then he fastened it very securely round the stump and went forward to the edge.

"Are you all right, Bertie?" he shouted.

"Quite right."

The face of the rock was very even, and there was nothing for the rope to chafe against. Harry lay down at the edge, keeping a firm hold of the rope to prevent himself from slipping over, and was able to look down on Bertie.

"Well, Bertie, what is it?"

"It is the wall of the house, I have no doubt, but it is so cleverly built that I can scarcely see where the arch ends and the house begins. Looking quite close I can see where the stones join, but their face has been left rough; and as it is just the same colour as the rocks, and lines have been cut down its face, and cracks made across it answering to the lines in the rock on both sides, I am sure I should not have known it was built up unless I had examined it. It is much narower on this side than on the other—not more than twenty-five feet, I should say. There seems to be some irregularly-shaped holes in what looks like a fissure in the middle. I suppose they are to light the rooms on this side of the house, but they are certainly too small to be noticed from the sea."

"Does the sea come right up to the foot of the cliff?"

It was a minute before the answer came. "The water comes to the foot, but there is a line of rocks running along forty or fifty feet farther out. Some of them seem to be thirty feet out of the water; at one end they touch the cliff, and at the other there is a free passage. The water is very clear, but as far as I can judge I should say there is a depth of a fathom or a fathom and a half between the rocks and the cliff. Certainly a boat could row into a position underneath where I am."

"Is there anything more?"

"No."

"You don't see an entrance down there?"

"No."

"All right! Then you may as well come up again. Can you climb up?"

"Easily."

"Well, hail me if you want me to haul."

Harry went back to the stump, unwound the rope until it was only half a turn round it, and then, holding it firmly, stood ready to haul up.

CHAPTER XI

INVESTIGATIONS

HARRY was relieved when, a few minutes later, Bertie's head appeared above the edge, and directly afterwards he crawled over.

"Well, so far so good, Bertie. There is no doubt that it is one of the best hiding-places in the world, and I am not a bit surprised that the Spaniards never found it. Now we will go back to the edge of the ravine and have a good look from that side."

As they went along he said, "Let us have a look at these bushes, Bertie. The soil is very thin about here, and I wonder that the trees grew."

"These are pines," Bertie said, "and in the mountains we often saw pines growing among rocks where there did not seem a handful of soil for them."

On examining they found several old stumps, and thrusting a ramrod down Harry found, to his surprise, that the soil was from three to four feet deep. He tried again a little farther off, and found that it was two feet; further still, it was only one.

"The tree must have stood in a hole in the rock," he said. "Try another one, Bertie." The same results were obtained. "That explains it, Bert. Evidently when they planted the trees to prevent this place from being seen from the hills, they cut away the rock in circles about twelve feet across and made cup-shaped holes, which they filled up with earth. When they planted the young trees I dare say at first they watered them. They could easily enough fetch water from the stream. When the trees got fairly rooted they would be able to leave them alone, perhaps giving them a good watering once every two or three months. Whenever the rains came they would be able to give up watering altogether, for in these basins the earth would keep moist for a very long time. It would be a big job, but no doubt the king who built the place had all his tribe at work on it. It is probable that the Incas had established themselves at Cuzco for many years before they came down to this place, and the trees may not have been planted till their coming was first heard of. In that case there would be plenty of time to hide the place before they came down and searched the shore. We know that the Chimoos resisted them for a considerable time before they were finally conquered. Well, for whatever purpose this place was built it is one in which either the Chimoos or the Incas, if they ever found the place, would be likely to hide treasure, which is satisfactory. Now we will sit down here for a short time and watch both windows. You look at the two top lines, Bertie, and I will look at the two lower lines. I certainly do not see any signs of life. That is how the water gets out," and he pointed to a roughly-shaped arch about twelve feet wide and as many high. Through this the little stream disappeared. "I expect there is a similar passage at the other end."

"There may have been," Bertie said. "I was hanging so close to the wall that there may very well have been one without my being able to see it. But it looks pitch-dark in there. If there were much of an opening we ought to see the light, for, as we agreed, it can't be more than a hundred feet long."

"That is the first place we will investigate, Bertie. The question of how we are to get into the house wants some thinking over. That lowest window is a good twenty-five feet above the ground."

"Of course if we had a grapnel we could fasten it to the end of a rope and chuck it in."

"We shall have to make something of that sort. If the window had been on the other side instead of this it would have been easy enough, because I could have lowered you and slipped down the rope afterwards, but that arch sticking out so far on this side makes it impossible. All that we can do now is, as far as I can see, to lower ourselves down on to the top of that wall in the ravine, then go and examine the tunnel. We have got plenty of rope to lower ourselves from here on to the wall."

They watched the building for another twenty minutes. "I am convinced that no one is there," Harry said. "I have not seen as much as a shadow pass any of the windows since. If people did live in it they would naturally be on this side of the house, because the rooms here are better lighted and more cheerful, and no doubt they are the principal rooms, as the house narrows so much at the other end."

They were above the wall, then, fastening the rope till they rose and walked along the edge of the ravine to a stump, they slid down on to it.

"So far so good, Harry said, as, holding their rifles in their hands, they went down the steps. Then he suddenly stopped. "Hullo," he exclaimed, "here are two skeletons!"

They were not quite skeletons, for the bones were covered by a parchment-like skin, and there were still remains of the short skirt each had worn in life. A spear lay beside each. With difficulty the brothers passed down without treading upon them.

"They must have been hear a long time, Harry," Bertie said when they got to the bottom.

"Any time," the other said. "In the dry air of these

low lands there is scarce any decay. You remember those mummies we saw. I believe iron or steel will lie here for years without rusting. They may have been here for a couple of hundred years or more."

"I wonder what killed them, Harry?"

"I have no idea. You see, one was lying almost on the other with his arms round his body, as if he had died trying to lift him up. If they had been shot by arrows they would still be sticking into them; if they had been killed by people pursuing them they would probably be lying upon their backs, for they naturally have faced round at the last moment to resist their pursuers, whereas there are no signs of injury. This settles the point that there is no one in the house. Had it been inhabited, the bodies would have been removed from the path, for it is by this that people would go out and return. There may have been a ladder down from the wall; the only other way they could have got out would have been through that passage to the sea. A boat may have been kept there; but even if that had been so, we should scarcely have found those bodies on the steps. Well, we shall have plenty of time to talk over that."

They walked across the open space until they approached the building. For a height of twenty feet it was constructed of stone, above that it appeared to be made of great adobe bricks which had been so largely used at Pachacamac, and in others of the old ruins they had seen.

"There is no question that it must have been built by the Chimoos or some race before them," Harry said; "the Incas could have had no possible reason for erecting such a place. Well, now for the tunnel."

The little stream only occupied two feet of the passage. They were therefore enabled to walk down dry-foot.

"We ought to have brought a torch with us," Bertie said.

"I don't think we shall want that; there is a sort of thin blue light, the reflection of the light upon the water outside, though I don't know why it should be so blue."

The reason was soon manifest. The passage sloped downwards, and when they had gone some fifty feet their progress was arrested by water which appeared of a deep-blue colour.

"That is it," Harry said. "You see the roof comes down into the water twenty feet off, and the light has come up under it. They sloped this passage to make the water flow out below the surface of the sea, so that the opening could not be seen from without. By the light I should not say the opening is more than six inches under the water. I don't know how the tides are, but if it is high tide now, the top of the opening would be eighteen inches out of the water at low tide, for, as you know, the tide only rises about two feet on this coast. In that case a boat would be able to come in and out at low tide, but of course a man wanting to come in or go out could easily dive under at any time. Well, that settles that point for the present. It was a clever plan; any amount of water could flow out in flood time, and yet no one who took the trouble to come behind that ledge of rocks we saw would have any idea that there was an opening. I think now that we had better go back, Bertie; in the first place because we can do nothing until we have manufactured a grapnel of some sort, and in the next place because every moment we delay will add to the anxiety of our friends in camp. We must have been away three hours, I should say."

They ascended the steps, fastened the short rope round a block at the top of the wall across the ravine, and lowered themselves down. They had to proceed with great care while making their way down the slope composed of rough and jagged rocks. Once at the bottom of the ravine, however, they walked briskly on. They had scarcely issued from the entrance when they saw a stir in the camp in the distance and heard a shout of delight, and then Dias dashed off to meet them at the top of his speed.

"Thanks to all the saints, señor, that you are safe! Have you been in the castle?"

"No, Dias we have not been in—for the good reason that we could not get in, because the only entrance is fully twenty-five feet from the ground. We cannot enter until we have made some contrivance by which a rope can be fixed there, or manufactured a ladder, which would be the best way and save a lot of trouble, if we could get a couple of poles long enough. We thought that we would come back when we had seen all there was to be seen outside the place."

The Indian's face fell. "Then you do not know what is in the house, señor?"

"No; but we are certain that there is no one there, and that probably no one has been there for the past two hundred years, and perhaps a good deal longer."

"And the demons have not interfered with you?"

"The demons knew better," Bertie laughed.

"They may not be powerful in the daytime," Dias said in an awed tone. "It is at night that they would be terrible."

"To-morrow we shall get inside, and Bertie and I will stop there all night, and if we neither see nor hear anything of them you may be quite sure that there are none there."

By this time they had arrived at the camp. "I knew you would came back safe, señors," Donna Maria said. "But what have you seen?"

"I see something now—or rather I don't see something now that I would like to see," Bertie laughed. "I thought you would have got a good dinner ready for me, but I do not see any signs of it being even begun."

The woman laughed. "I have been too busy keeping up Dias's spirits. I will set about getting dinner at once."

"No, no," Harry said; "we are really not hungry. We had a good meal before we started. So do you three sit down and I will tell you all we have seen."

The three natives listened with intense interest. When he had done, Maria clapped her hands. "It must be a wonderful place," she said. "I wish I had gone with you. I will go tomorrow if you will take me."

"Certainly we will take you, Maria; and I have no doubt that Dias will go too."

"I will go as far as the place," said Dias, "but I will not promise to go in."

"I won't press you, Dias. When we have slept there a night I have no doubt you will become convinced that it is quite safe. And now about the ladder. We shall really want two to be comfortable—one for getting up to the window, that must be made of wood; the other, which will be used for getting up and down the wall in the ravine, may be made of ropes. But I think that that had best be hung from the top of the ravine above it, so as to avoid having to climb over those rough stones at the foot, which are really awkward. One might very well twist one's ankle among them."

"I will go at once, señor, and get the poles," Dias said. "You may as well come with me, Jose. We passed a wood in the valley about five miles off; there we can cut down a couple of young trees. If we put the saddles on two of the riding mules, when we have got the poles clear we can fasten the ends to ropes and trail them behind us."

"We shall also want some of the branches you cut off,

Dias. You had better say thirty lengths of about two feet long, so that we may place the rungs nine inches apart. You had better get poles thirty feet long, for we may not have just the height by a couple of feet."

The two natives at once rode off, and the brothers set to work to collect sticks for the fire.

"It is too bad, señors, that this should not have been done while you were away, but we thought of nothing but your danger."

"You were perfectly right, Maria; if we were in peril, you did the best thing of all to obtain help for us. As to the dinner, there is no hurry whatever for it. What have you got to eat?"

"There is nothing, señor, but a few of the fish we fried two days ago, and the ham that we smoked of that bear."

"I will take the line, then, and go down and try to catch some fresh fish," Bertie said. "There is a good-sized pool about half-way between here and the ravine. I might get some fish there."

"I will take my gun, Bertie, and go up to the bushes by the ravine, and see if I can get a bird or two. There is no other shelter anywhere about here."

In half an hour the lad brought a dozen fish into the camp. None of them were above half a pound, but they were nearly of a size.

"These will be very nice," the woman said with a smile as he handed them to her. "I have thrown away the others. I do not think we dried them enough; they were certainly going bad. I have heard your brother fire several times, and as he does not often miss, I have no doubt he will bring us something."

Twenty minutes later Harry was seen coming along. When he arrived he threw down a large bunch of wild pigeons.

"There are ten brace," he said. "That will give us four apiece."

Dias and José soon arrived at a gallop, with the long poles trailing behind them and a fagot of short sticks fastened to each saddle.

"Those are capital poles, Dias," Harry said as he examined them—"strong enough for anything. We will chop notches in them for the rungs to lie in. There will be no fear then of their shifting, which they might do if the lashings stretched. Now, we have got a capital dinner just done to a turn, so you see we have not been lazy while you were away."

As soon as the meal was finished they set to work to make the ladder. A short stick was cut as a guide to the space that was to be left between the rungs. Bertie and José marked off the distances on the two poles, and Dias and Harry with their axes cut the grooves in which the sticks were to lie. Then the poles were laid a foot apart, and the work of pressing the sticks into their places began. They agreed that the ropes should not be cut up, as they would be wanted for fastening on the loads whenever the mules went to fetch food or powder. Two of the head-ropes were used on each side, and a firm job was made.

"When you go, Dias, for the powder and so on, you must get another supply of rope. We shall want a longer ladder than this in the ravine, and also a rope to lift powder and firewood and so on into the castle, and perhaps for other things that one does not think of at present. Tomorrow we will unfasten the cord by which we descended to the wall, as we shall not want to use that in future. I think tomorrow, when we go to the castle, as you and José do not mean to accompany us, you might take your axes and cut down a lot of those stumps among the brushwood, split them up, and pitch them into the court yard of the castle. It would be well to lay in a good stock of firewood. We shall want it for cooking and lighting of an evening. We have only one or two torches left, and we shall want a cheerful fire."

"I may go with you tomorrow, may I not?" Maria said.

"Certainly you may if you wish."

"I should like to," she said. "In your company I shan't be a bit afraid of demons; and I want to see the place."

"If Maria goes I will go," Dias said. "I don't like it; but if she went and I didn't I should never hear the last if it."

The next morning they moved the mules and all their belongings to the extreme end of the valley. Then they had an early breakfast. José took up his axe and the others their arms; the former turned back for the point where he could climb the hill. Dias and Harry took the heavy end of the ladder, Bertie the light one, and they started up the ravine. Maria followed with a store of bread that she had baked the day before. It was hard work carrying the ladder up the rocks at the foot of the wall. When it was securely fastened there, they mounted and dragged it up to them.

As soon as the ladder was in position Harry mounted, closely followed by Bertie. Dias hesitated; but a merry laugh from his wife settled the point, and he followed with an expression of grave determination on his face. As soon as he was on the ladder his wife followed him with a light step.

As Harry reached the top, he found that the sill of the window was two feet and a half above the floor of the apartment. He stepped down and then looked round. The room occupied the whole width of the house, and was some twenty feet wide. Four rows of pillars ran across it, supporting the roof above. The ends of the room were in semi-darkness. It was not above ten feet in height. There were rude carvings on the pillars and the walls.

By the time he had made these observations the others had joined him. "I see people there," Dias said, in an awed voice, pointing to one end of the room. Harry dropped the barrel of his rifle into the palm of his left hand. After gazing two seconds he placed it on his shoulder, saying, "There are people, Dias, but they won't do us any harm;" and he walked in that direction. Two figures lay on the ground; four others were in a sitting position, close to each other, against the end wall. Some bows and arrows and spears lay near them. All were dressed in a garment of rough cloth. Harry walked up to one and touched it on the head with the muzzle of his gun. As he did so it crumbled away; the bones rattled on the stone floor as they fell. Donna Maria gave a little cry. "They are dead" she exclaimed. "They must have been dead years and years ago."

"Two or three hundred, I should think. Your legends are evidently true, Dias. There was a party left here to keep strangers from entering this place. Now, before we go farther, let us think this out. We will sit down on the ledge of the window. But before we do so, take a good look at their arms and skulls, Dias. You have often been with travellers to the ruins; let us hear what you say."

Dias, who was now assured that he had only to deal with human beings, examined them carefully, looking at the ornaments that still hung round their necks, and then said: "They are not the old people, señor; these were Incas."

"That is an important point; now let us see how this is to be explained. Now," he said, as they sat down, "it is clear that the Incas did know this building. They may have discovered treasures here or they may not; but it would certainly seem that they were as anxious as the Chimoos had been to keep its existence a secret, and it is certain that they must have had some interest in doing so. We have reason to believe that the Spaniards at least did not know of it. There is no doubt whatever that these men were not killed in fight; on the contrary, their sitting position proves that they died quietly, and probably at the same time. We see no signs of food; we may find some as we search the place. If we do not, we must take it that they either died from an outbreak of some epidemic or from hunger. And it is quite probable that the two skeletons on the steps were two of their companions who were going out to seek for food, and that they fell from weakness; one clearly died in the act of trying to lift the other. What do you think of that, Dias?"

"I think what you say is likely. But why should they have died from hunger?"

"It is probable that others were in the secret, and were in the habit of bringing provisions to them, and perhaps of relieving them at certain periods. We know that there were fierce battles in the early times of the Spaniards. In one of these battles the whole of those who were aquainted with the secret may have fallen. Or it may have been earlier after the conquest had been completed, when the Spaniards drove tens of thousands of men to work as slaves in the mines. The people here may have remained at their post, hoping for relief until it was too late. Two of the strongest may have started at last, but have been too weak to climb the steps, and died there. Their comrades may have never known their fate, but have sat down to die here, as you see. I should think it probable that the second of my suggestions is likely to be the right one, and that this did not take place until perhaps a hundred years after the arrival of the

Spaniards, otherwise those legends of men who came near this place being killed would never have been handed down. If all this is as I suggest, either the Incas knew that the Chimoos had buried treasure here, or they themselves buried some, although, as you say, there is no tradition of treasure having been taken here. But it is possible that that treasure ship, which undoubtedly sailed from some place along the coast and was never again heard of, really came here; that her treasure was landed, and the vessel then destroyed. In either case, there is a strong reason for hope that there is treasure somewhere in this castle if we can but find it."

"We will find it," Bertie said confidently. "What you say must be true. These Indians would never have been fools enough to sit here and die without some good reason for it. Well, I vote that before we do anything else we clear these bones out."

"We can do that the first thing tomorrow morning, Bertie. We can't just throw them out of the window. The bones are of men who died doing their duty to their country. We will leave them as they are today, and tomorrow we will bring up one of the big leather bags, place the bones in it, and take them down into the valley and bury them."

"Then you won't sleep here tonight, Harry?"

"No; I have not a shadow of superstition, but I do not think it would be lively here with those things at the end of the room. Now, let us look about a bit.

"This was evidently the great hall of the place; do you not think so, Dias?"

"Yes, señor; the house gets narrower as it nears the sea. This is by far the best lighted room on this side. No doubt the rooms on this floor were the abode of the chief who built it, and his principal followers; the others would be above."

"Well, we will light the two torches. Yes, there is no doubt that this was the room. You see there are brackets against all the pillars for holding torches. Before we go farther we will see what they are made of."

He took his knife out of his pocket and went up to one of the brackets, which consisted of bars of metal an inch and a half square and eighteen inches long. They widened out at the end, and here was a round hole about two inches in diameter, evidently intended to put the torch in. The metal was black with age. He scraped a few inches off one of them with his knife. "Silver!" he exclaimed. "It would have been better if they had been gold. But as there are four on each pillar, and twelve pillars, they would make a tidy weight. That is a good beginning, Bertie. If they are the same in all the rooms there would be several tons of it."

There was but one door to the room; through this they passed. Dias, now that there was some explanation for what he considered the work of the demons, had a more assured air. One passage led straight on; two others ran parallel to the wall of the room they had left.

"We will examine these first," Harry said. "It is likely enough they lead to the stairs to the lower room. There must be two floors below us, one above the level of the top of the tunnel, the other below that must be divided in two by it."

As they advanced into the passage there was a strange and sudden clamour, a roaring sound mingled with sharp shrieks and strange little piping squeaks. Maria ran back with a shriek of alarm, and there was a strange rush overhead. The torches were both extinguished and Harry and his brother discharged their rifles almost at the same moment. Dias burst into a shout of laughter as they both dropped their weapons and swung their double-barrelled guns forward. "What on earth is it, Dias?"

"It is bats and birds, señor. I have seen them come out of caves that way many times. I dare say the place is full of bats. The birds would only come into rooms where there is some light."

Turning round they saw quite a cloud of bats flying out through the door.

"Confound it!" Harry said. "They have given me the worst fright I ever had in my life."

They went back to the room they had left. Both Harry and Bertie had lost every tinge of colour from their faces.

"I am very glad, Harry," Bertie said, with an attempt at a laugh, "that you were frightened. I was scared almost out of my life."

"Ah, señors," Dias said triumphantly, "you thought they were demons!"

"I did not think they were demons, Dias, but what they were I could not tell you. I never heard any such sound before. I am not ashamed to say that I did feel badly frightened."

CHAPTER XII

THE SEARCH BEGINS

In a few minutes all were ready to go on again. This time they found everything perfectly quiet in the passage. Two or three yards beyond the spot at which they had before arrived they saw a staircase to the left. It was faintly lighted from above, and, mounting it, they found themselves in a room extending over the whole width and depth of the house. The roof at the eastern end was not supported by pillars, but by walls three feet wide and seven or eight feet apart. The first line of these was evidently over the wall of the room they had left. There were four lines of similar supports erected, they had no doubt, over the walls of rooms below. The light from the four windows in front, and from an irregular opening at the other end some three feet high and six inches wide, afforded sufficient light for them to move about without difficulty. There were many signs of human habitation here. Along the sides were the remains of mats, which had apparently divided spaces six feet wide into small apartments. Turnings these over they found many trifles—arrow-heads, bead-necklaces, fragments of pots, and even a child's doll.

"I expect this is the room where the married troops lived and slept," Harry said; "there is not much to see here."

The two stories above were exactly similar, except that there were no remains of dividing mats nor of female ornaments. They walked to the narrow end. Here the opening for light was of a different shape from those in the rooms below. It had apparently been originally of the same shape, but had been altered. In the middle it was like the others, three feet high and six inches wide, but a foot from the bottom there was a wide cut, a foot high and three feet wide. As they approached it Dias gave an exclamation of surprise. Two skeletons lay below it. "They must have been on watch here, señor, when they died," he said as they came up to them.

"It is a rum place to watch," Bertie said, "for you cannot see out."

"You are right, Bertie, it is a curious hole."

The wall was over two feet thick; all the other openings had been driven straight through it, and, as they had noticed, were doubtless made in the stones before they were placed there, for inside they were cleanly cut, and it was only within three inches of the outer face that the edges had been left rough. This opening was of quite a different character. It sloped at a sharp angle, and no view of the open sea could be obtained, but only one of the line of rocks at the foot of the cliffs. It was roughly made, and by the marks of the tools, probably of hardened copper, it had evidently been cut from the inside.

Harry stood looking for some time. "I cannot understand their cutting the hole like this. It could not be noticed from the sea that there was an opening at all; that is plain enough. But why make the hole at all when you can see nothing from it? And yet a watch has been placed here, while there was none at the other places where they could make out any passing ship."

"Perhaps," Bertie said, "it was done in order that if from the other places boats were seen approaching, they could chuck big stones down from here and sink any boat that might row inside the rocks into the entrance to the passage, which, as this is in the middle of the room, must be just under us."

"In that case they would have kept a supply of big stones here. I have no doubt whatever that it was made some time after the castle was built, and I should say, judging by its unfinished state, the work was done in haste. But what for, goodness only knows. Well now, having made no discoveries whatever on the upper floor, we will go down. It is certain that there can be no great treasure hidden under any of these floors, there is not depth enough for hiding-places. I counted the steps as we came upstairs, and there cannot be much more than two feet between the floor of one room and the ceiling in the next. I fancy that this is of single stones, each the flooring length of the space between the half-walls. You see that there is a long beam of stone running on the top of the dividing wall, and the ends of these stones appear to rest on it. It is below that we must look for hiding-places."

They descended to the first floor. They found that the space behind the great room was divided into a number of chambers. All of these, with the exception of the small one of the sea-face, were necessarily in absolute darkness, and in all were brackets for torches, similar to those in the principal chamber. Bertie counted them, and found that, including those first met with, they numbered one hundred and twenty-three.

"How much do you think they weigh apiece?" he asked Harry when the tour was finished.

"I have not the slightest idea, Bertie. I should think about fifteen pounds, but it may be five pounds less than that. They would certainly give a very nasty knock on the head."

"Oh, I was not thinking of knocks on the head. If there are a hundred bars at fifteen pounds apiece, it is a big amount of silver; if they are only ten pounds each —and really I think that is nearer the mark—they weigh a thousand pounds. What is silver worth a pound?"

"It varies. You can put it at five shillings an ounce; that would be three pounds sterling for one of silver— three thousand pounds in a rough calculation for the lot."

"Well that is not a bad beginning, Harry; it would pay all the expenses and leave a couple of thousand over."

Harry shrugged his shoulders. "A drop in the ocean as far as I am concerned, Bertie. Still, it is a beginning; and you may be sure that they did not take all of this trouble to guard this castle for the sake of three thousand pounds' worth of silver."

They now went down to the next floor. Here there were two staircases, and the space was divided into two parts by a wall along the centre. There were no openings whatever for light. One half had evidently been devoted to arms. Here still lay hundreds of spear-shafts, tens of thousands of arrows, piles of hide shields, and caps of the same material.

"This store must have been larger than was required for the garrison of the place," Harry said, "it must have been a reserve for re-arming a whole tribe."

Besides the arms there were great bales of rough cloth and piles of skins, all in a marvellous state of preservation owing to the dryness of the air. After thoroughly examining the room they went up the stair leading into it and descended those into the adjoining chamber. This was divided into compartments by transverse walls four feet shorter than the width, thereby leaving a passage through from end to end. Here in confusion—for the most part turned inside out—were sacks of matting and

may have passed before the last of the garrison died of hunger, and probably all others who were in the secret fell in some insurrection or died in the mines. All this seems plain enough, except that possibly there was no treasure. That left by the Chimoos may have been discovered by the Incas. I should think it extremely likely that the ship Dias mentioned as setting out with a large amount of treasure was intended to land its stores here.

"It may have done so, it may have sunk at sea. I am inclined to think that it was lost, because the traditions concerning these hidden treasures seem to be extremely accurate; and yet, as Dias says, none tell of any Inca treasure being concealed here. However, it is quite possible the treasure did come here and was landed, and that the ship was then broken up, so that it might be supposed she was lost at sea, and that this was kept so profound a secret by the men here, that the news was never generally known even among the natives. So far our search to-day has been successful, but I see that a hunt for the treasure will be a very difficult one. Certainly in the upper chambers there doesn't appear any possibility of such a hiding-place existing. The whole space is accounted for. The walls are all of solid stone, and have no special thickness. If the roofs had been arched there might be empty spaces on each side of the spring of the arch, but they are supported by pillars or walls, with only just space between the floors for the beams of solid stone. Of course it is in the lowest room that one would expect to find hiding-places like those we saw at Pachacamac." He paused.

"Well, why should they not be there, Harry?"

"Because, as we saw, the floor is at most twelve inches above the water-level. How is it possible that they could have constructed chambers below that level, that is in the bed of a torrent? It is probable that the solid rock lies many feet below the bed of the stream. A portion of that great arch must from time to time have fallen into it; it may be that the river once ran forty or fifty feet below its present level. In all the places that we have seen these treasure chambers were formed in solid adobe foundations, as the temples always stood on artificial terraces. With all our appliances at the present time it would be next to impossible to sink in a stratum of great rock fragments below the water-level, and I do not believe that the old people here could have done so even had it been a solid rock. The difficulties of excavating chambers in it would have been enormous. They could split rocks with the grain, and all the stone walls we have seen were made of regular pieces, and evidently formed of stone so split. They were able to give them a sort of facing with great labour, but the tools they had were not made of material hard enough to work in solid rock, and the labour of excavating such chambers would have been stupendous. Therefore I am at a loss to imagine where any such chambers can be in that castle."

Dias nodded gravely. He had been with travellers who had done a great deal of excavation, and he was able to understand Harry's argument. Maria, who was listening attentively, also understood it. José simply rolled cigarettes and smoked them. It was a matter for his elders, and he did not even try to follow what Harry was saying. There was some minutes' silence, and then Bertie said, "But the floors are all even."

"What do you mean, Bertie?" Harry asked in a puzzled tone.

"I mean, Harry, that they run straight along. There is no dip in them."

"Of course there isn't. Who ever heard of building floors on the slope?"

"Yes, that is what I mean. We know that the tunnel

slopes down its own height. It is twelve feet high at the entrance, and at the lower end it is some inches below the level, so it falls twelve feet at least. At the end where the cistern is, the floor of the basement is only a few inches above the bottom of the passage; therefore at the other end it must be twelve feet above the water-level."

"You are right, Bertie!" Harry exclaimed. "What a fool I was not to think of it! There must be a space underneath it a hundred feet long, sloping from nothing down to twelve feet. There is room for a dozen chambers such as those we saw on each side of the tunnel. Well done Bertie you have given me fresh hope. It would be a splendid hiding-place, for any searchers who came down and saw the water in the cistern would believe at once that, as neither the Chimoos nor the Incas could have known how to build under water, there was no use in searching for hidden chambers under this floor. You see, neither of them had any knowledge of cement or mortar. All their bricks and stones are laid without anything of the sort; and whatever amount of labour was available no chamber could be made under water, for as fast as holes were dug the water would come in, and even if they could line it with stone-work the water would penetrate through the cracks. Now, Dias, that we see with certainty where we have to dig we can make our preparations. I will write down a list of the things we decided the other day we should want:—Six kegs of powder, two hundred feet of fuse, four boring-tools, six steel wedges, the smallest smith's fire you can buy—for we shall have to sharpen the tools,—six borers, a large bundle of torches, four sledge-hammers—we have enought pickaxes and shovels,—and another fifty fathoms, that is a hundred yards, of rope. I don't know anything else that we shall want in the mining way.

"You and your wife had better settle what provisions

you must get. We shall certainly need a good supply of flour—a couple of sacks, I should think—tea, coffee, and sugar, dried or salted meat. And you might get a supply of smoked fish. I have no doubt that we shall catch fresh fish here in the sea, but we shall all be too busy to spend much time on that. You had better get three or four gallons of pulque; one cannot be always drinking coffee. We have still got a good supply of whisky and brandy. Your wife will certainly want a good supply of red pepper and other things for her stews. It would not be a bad thing to have a couple of crates of poultry. Don't pack them too closely, or half of them will be smothered before you get them here. Dead meat will be of no use, for it won't keep in this heat. We can turn them all out in the courtyard in front of the castle, and they can pick up their living there among the lower slopes of the cliffs. We can give them a few handfuls of grain a day. Don't get too many cocks, and let the hens be young ones. They ought to supply us with plenty of eggs and some broods of chickens. You must calculate what the weight will be, and take the mules accordingly."

"Very well, señor. I need not be away more than three days at most. It is only twenty miles to Ancon."

"You might take the two llamas down with you and sell them there. They have done good work, and I should not like to kill and eat them. So mind you sell them to someone who wants them for carriage work. We shall not require them any more for that purpose. Will you want to take José with you?"

"I think not, señor, for I should say that four baggage mules will be ample, and I can lead them myself; and certainly you will find José useful here."

Dias and his wife then withdrew a short distance from the fire, and engaged in an animated conversation as to the things she required.

"Don't stint matters," Harry said, raising his voice. "We may be here for the next two or three months, and the less frequently you have to go down to buy things the better. It would be easy to account for your first purchases by saying that you were going on an expedition to the mountains, but you could not go to the place with the same story again."

"There are two places I can go to, señor; but I will get a good store of everything this time."

Dias started at daybreak with four mules and the two llamas. The others rolled up the tent-beds and the remaining stores, loaded up the other mules, and moved down to the mouth of the ravine. Here they pitched the little tents again.

"They will form a central point for the mules to come to," Harry said. "We will leave the sacks of maize here, but give the animals a good feed now. They will be sure to keep close to the spot. All the other things we will carry into the castle; but before we start we will bury these bags of bones."

When this was done, and the saddles taken off and piled together against the rocks, the other things were made up in portable packets, and they started up the ravine. They made three journeys before everything was brought to the foot of the ladder leading up to the window. Then the two brothers mounted, and hauled the things up with a rope which José, who remained below, fastened to them. When the last was up he went to the foot of the rock and brought several armfuls of the wood he had thrown down on the previous day. This was also hauled up.

"You had better fetch some more, José. We mean to keep a big fire burning here night and day; it will make the place cheerful. I will have a fire also burning where we are at work below. Now, señora, we will rig up some blankets on a line between the pillars at the end of the room opposite to that in which we found the skeletons, so as to make a special apartment for you and Dias. We will spread our beds at night near the fire."

The screen was soon made. A cord was run from the wall to the pillar next to it, some five feet above the floor, and three blankets were sufficient to fill the space.

Harry was about to make another line from the pillar, when Maria said:

"I would rather not, señor; I am not a bit afraid. This screen is quite large enough, and it will be more cheerful not to be shut up altogether, as then, when I am lying down, I can see the reflection of the fire on the walls, and it will be much more cheerful."

Then a blazing fire was lit. The wood was almost dry as tinder, and burnt without smoke. It was built almost touching the back wall, in which some five feet above the fire, Harry with a pick made a hole four inches deep.

While he was doing this, José went down and cut a sapling four inches in diameter, growing in a cleft on the rock, and from this cut off two six-foot lengths and brought them up. One end of the thickest of these was driven into the hole and tightly wedged in there, the other end was lashed securely to an upright beam.

"There, Maria," he said when it was finished, "you will be able to hang your pots and kettles from that at any height you like above the fire. Now, you can set to work as soon as you like, to get breakfast for us. We have been at work for four or five hours, and have good appetites."

"I have the cakes ready to bake, señor, and I shan't be long before I get an olla ready for you."

"Well, José what do you think of the place?" Harry asked.

"I should like it better if it were not so big," the lad said. "I shall want a broom, señor, to sweep out the dust."

"It is three inches deep," Maria said.

"I should not bother about that, Maria; it would be a tremendous job to sweep such a big room, and the dust is so fine that it would settle again and cover everything. Besides, it will be a good deal softer to lay our beds on than the stones would be, so I think you had better let it remain as it is, especially as you are fond of going about without your shoes. I think I will rig up a blanket against the doorway. It will make the place look a good deal more snug, and will keep the bats from returning."

"I am not afraid of the bats, now I know what they are; but I should be constantly expecting them to rush out again."

"I expect a good many went back last night," Harry said. "We won't put the blankets up till after dark. They are sure to come out again; then as soon as they have gone, we will close it, and they won't be able to get in when they come back before daybreak."

Harry's expectations were fulfilled. At dusk a stream of bats rushed out again, but this time quite noiselessly. The rush lasted for three or four minutes. As soon as they had gone, the blankets were hung up, and fastened across the doorway.

"They will be puzzled when they come back."

"Yes, señor," Maria said; "but when they find that they can't get in here, they will come in through the openings above."

"So they will; I did not think of that. But when they once find that they cannot get out here in the evening, they will go out where they came in, and we shall have no more trouble with them."

They were all roused just before dawn by a squeaking and twittering noise. They threw on fresh logs, and as these blazed up they could see a cloud of bats flying overhead. They kept on going to the doorway, and when they found they could not get through they retired with angry squeaks. The light was gradually breaking, and in a few minutes all had flown out through the opening. Harry and his brother followed them, and could see them flitting about the upper windows. Presently, as if by a common impulse, they poured in through the various openings.

"I don't suppose we shall see any more of them," Harry said, "and I own that I shall be glad. There is something very weird in their noiseless flitting about, and in the shadows the fire casts on the ceiling."

After drinking a cup of coffee, with a small piece of maize cake, Bertie said:

"What is the programme for today?"

"We can't do much till Dias comes back. We may as well go down and have a look at the lower rooms. I don't think there is much dust on the floor there, but while José is away looking after the mules we will cut enough bushes to make a couple of brooms. We shall want the place swept as clean as possible, so that we can look about, but I don't think there is the least chance of our being able to move the stones. Before we do anything we will go down to the pool and have a swim, and dive out through the entrance and have a look at those rocks."

"That is right," Bertie said. "I was longing for one yesterday morning, but of course the first thing to be done was to examine this place."

"Would it be safe for me to bathe, señor?"

"Quite safe, Maria; the slope is very gradual, and you need have no fear of getting out of your depth suddenly. We will be off at once, Bertie."

CHAPTER XIII

AT WORK

HARRY and his brother went to the edge of the pool, where they undressed and waded out. They found that the bottom of the passage sloped more gradually at the edge of the water than it did higher up, and they were able to walk out till they came to the point where the roof dipped into the water. They dived, and in a few strokes came up beyond the roof.

"This is glorious!" Bertie said. "We have often bathed in pools, but this is a different thing altogether. It is more than a year since we had our last dip in the sea, the day we arrived at Callao."

Although there was little or no wind, the rollers were breaking on the line of rocks outside, pouring over the lower points in volumes of foam, and coming in broken waves up the passage.

"We mustn't go beyond the point, Bertie or we may be dashed against the foot of the cliff. We will climb that rock to the left; it is not too steep, and I think we can manage it. From there we shall get a good view of this side of the house and of the situation in general."

It required considerable care to climb the rocks, and more than once they hurt their feet on sharp projections. The top of the rock, however, was smooth by the action of time and sea, and they were able to sit down on it in comfort.

"The castle is just as you described it, Bertie; and certainly no one sailing past, however close he came outside these rocks, would be able to detect it. No doubt the stone of which it is built is the same as that of the cliffs. Most likely it was taken from the ravine where the passage now is, and had fallen from the arch above. It might have been more noticeable at first, but now it is weathered into exactly the same tint as the cliffs. The openings are very dodgily placed, and a stranger would not dream that they went many inches in. Now, from where we stand we can look up into that curious opening on the top story. I have been puzzling over that ever since I saw it, but can't think of any possible reason for its having been cut like that, except to enable them to throw stones on to any boat that came into this passage behind the rocks; and yet that can hardly have been the case, for, as I remarked, there are no stones piled up there. Certainly they had a very large number of arrows, but stones would be very much more useful than arrows against a boat almost under their feet. However, that does not concern us now. This line of rocks must greatly aid in hiding the house from the sea. They are higher than you thought they were, looking down at them from above. We are quite thirty feet above the water, and at two or three points they are at least ten or twelve feet higher. Of course a short way out no one would be able to see that they were detached from the cliff, or that there was any passage whatever behind them.

"Besides, they break the force of the waves. If it was not for them it would be impossible for any boat to come up close to the face of the house, and a heavy storm might even break down the wall altogether. A tremendous sea would roll in here in a westerly gale; and if it hadn't been for these rocks it would have been necessary to build the lower part of the house absolutely solid to resist the sea. It is possible that the rocks were higher than they now are when the place was first constructed, in which case the house might have been almost entirely hidden from sight. Well, we may as well go back again, Bertie; we know all there is to be known about this side."

They swam back into the tunnel, dressed, and went out.

"We have come out, Maria," Bertie called. "The coast is clear for you. The water is not so deep as we thought it was, and you can walk out to the point where the roof comes down on to the water without getting out of your depth."

It did not take them long to cut a number of switches to serve as brooms, and a couple of handles. They carried them up into the house, and lashed the switches firmly on to the handles. The work was rough, but the brooms when completed were large, and, although not strong enough for heavy work, would do well to sweep aside the thin layer of almost impalpable dust on the floor below.

"Shall we take wood down there, Harry?"

"No; I think a fire would be a drawback rather than an assistance. It would be very valuable if we were working at one spot, but it could give no general light in a place a hundred feet long. We will take a torch down, and hold it and sweep by turns. We shall only want, to begin with, to make a clear path a couple of feet wide down the middle. Of course later on we shall clear it all. That will be sufficient to enable us to see how the floor is constructed, whether with big blocks or small ones, how closely they are fitted together, and so on. It is certainly unlikely that we shall find any indication as to where chambers exist."

It took but a very short time to clear the path; the dust was so light that one sweep of the broom cleared it away. When they got to the farther end they returned to examine the floor. For four or five feet from the cistern the rock had been evidently untouched, except to cut off any projecting points. Then there was a clear line running across the path. Bertie held the torch down close to it. Harry knelt down and examined it.

"This is a clean cut, Bertie. It is evidently solid above this, but the stone is not quite the same colour on each side of it, and it looks as if they had cut away the rock here and begun to build so as to keep the floor level. The cut may be six inches deep and it may be a foot, that doesn't matter The face of this stone is very smooth, but it is not cut; it is, I think, the face of the natural fracture. Move the torch along and let us see where the next join is. Ah, here it is!"

The slab was four feet across.

"You had better sweep the dust off both ways, Bertie, so that we may see what size it is."

It was, they found, about eight feet long.

"It has straight edges, Harry, almost as straight as if it had been sawn."

"Very likely it was sawn, Bertie; They could have had no tools that would cut a hard stone like this regularly, but as they were certainly clever builders they must have employed some means to do it. Possibly they used a saw without teeth, for however much they might have hardened the copper, the teeth could not have stood, but if they had a hard copper band fixed like the saw some masons use, and kept the stone moistened with fine sand, they might have cut into it. Of course it would have been a slow process; but they would not have needed to go far into the stone, for when they got down two or three inches they might have broken it through by dropping a heavy weight on the end. It would not have mattered if the fracture had not been straight below the cut, for only on the surface would they have wanted to fit accurately to the next stone. In another way they might have got a straight edge, that is, by driving very dry wedges into the cut made by the saw, and then moistening them. I know that great stones can be split in that way. They may have used both methods. However it doesn't matter to us much how they did it. It is clear that they could in some way or other cut stones. As they took the trouble to do so here, we may conclude that they were anxious to have a smooth floor that would be extremely difficult to get up.

"They would never have taken all this trouble if they had been merely making a floor for a cellar. For that purpose it would only have been necessary to throw rocks and stones of all sizes into the vacant space below, and when it was nearly full, to level it with small stones and sand. That they chose to undertake such tremendous labour as the making of so regular a floor as this must have been, shows that they had some very strong motive for doing so."

Going carefully along the track they had cleared, they found that the stones were of different sizes; some were but two feet wide, others as much as ten, but all fitted so closely together that it was difficult to see the joints.

"It is going to be a hard job to get these out, Bertie," Harry said, when they had completed their examination, "and it is lucky for us that the room gradually narrows from sixteen feet wide to two at the other end, and when we stepped it we made it eighty feet long. We need not take up the stones near the rock wall, for the ravine would naturally narrow as it went lower, and the depth would be greatest by the side of the wall of the tunnel."

"Well, we shall soon blow up the stones when we have got the powder."

"I hope so, Bertie; but I see that we shall have difficulty unless these top stones are extraordinarily thick."

Bertie looked surprised. "Why, I should have thought

the thicker they were the more difficult to break up."

"Beyond a certain point that would be so. But suppose they are six inches thick, you may take it for granted that underneath there will be rubble, loose stuff, except where any chambers may be built. If we were to bore a hole through this top layer the powder, instead of splitting the stones up, would expend its force among the loose stuff beneath it; and besides, instead of remaining in its place, it might get scattered, and we would then get no explosion at all."

"Then we should only have to make the hole four inches deep, Harry?"

"As a result of which there would only be two inches of tamping over the powder, and this would blow right out, as if from a little mortar, and would have no effect whatever upon the stone. I have no doubt that we shall find some way to get over these difficulties, but it is evident that the work will not be all clear sailing."

"Of course we shall manage it somehow, Harry, even if we have to smash up all the stones with the sledge-hammers Dias will bring us."

"Is breakfast nearly ready, señora? That swim in the sea has given us a prodigious appetite. Did you enjoy it?"

Maria nodded.

"It is very nice, señor; but I should have liked it better if the water had not been so blue. It seems so strange bathing in blue water."

"You will soon get accustomed to it," Bertie laughed. "There are no pools except that one two miles up the valley. Besides, it is much nicer to have a great bathing chamber all to yourself. Here comes José!"

"Well, José, are the mules all right?" he shouted.

"Yes, but I had difficulty in catching them. They had evidently been frightened by something, and were three miles up the valley with their coats all staring. It must have been either a puma or a jaguar. Of course they must have got wind of him in time; but as, fortunately, they were not tethered, they were able to get away from him."

"I should think he must be up somewhere among the bushes, José," Harry said. "We had better go down to-night and see if he returns again. We shall be losing some of the mules if we don't put a stop to his marauding. Besides it will be very dangerous for you, José, cutting the wood up there, if he is lurking somewhere. It is fortunate that you escaped yesterday."

"I expect he was on the other side of the ravine, señor; and even if he had not been, the sound of the chopping would have scared him. They will not often attack in the daytime."

When they had finished their breakfast José asked what he should do next.

"There is nothing else to do, so it would be as well to take our pickaxes and get some of those brackets out of the walls. We will begin with the other rooms of this floor and leave these here till the last."

"I will come and hold a torch for you, señors," Maria said. "I like to be doing something. I will wash up first, and then I shall have nothing to do till it is time to get ready for dinner. Now I know there is a savage beast about I should not like to go down the ladder."

"There is very little chance of his coming down the rocks," Harry said. "He is more likely to be lying somewhere on the other side watching the mules."

No move was made until the woman was ready to start. Then they lit two torches. She took one and Bertie the other, while José and Harry took two picks. It was hard work, for the brackets were driven far into the pillars and walls. It was necessary to knock away the stones round them to a depth of two or three inches before they could be got out. They worked one at each side of a bracket, relieving each other by turns, and after four hours' work only eighteen brackets had been got out. As far as they could tell by lifting them, the weight was somewhat greater than they had at first supposed. Harry could hold one out in each hand for a minute and a half, Bertie and José for a little over half a minute, and they agreed that they must be about twenty pounds each.

By this time their shoulders ached, and it was agreed that they had done a good day's work. For the rest of the day they did nothing but sit on the sill of the window and smoke quietly. The next day's work was similar, and twenty more brackets were got out. Late in the afternoon they saw Dias coming down the steps, and at once went down the ladder to meet him.

"Have you got everything, Dias?"

"I think so, señor, and I can tell you that the mules have had a pretty heavy load to bring back."

"Well, we will go with you at once, Dias, and bring some of the things up. I expect you have had nothing to eat since the morning. Before you do anything else you had better go in. Your wife has been keeping a dish hot for you, as she did not know when you might arrive."

"I shall not be long before I come and help you, señor. I have unsaddled the mules and turned them out to graze."

"It is just as well, Dias, for there is a beast somewhere about that gave them a fright last night. We will get all the eatables up tonight, the powder and drills and hammers we can very well leave till tomorrow morning."

It took them four trips to bring the provisions over, for it required two of them to carry each sack of flour, and indeed all had to give their aid in getting them up the rocky slope at the foot of the wall.

"No one seemed to think it unusual, your taking so

large a load, I hope, Dias?" Harry said as they sat down to their evening meal.

"No, señor. The man I bought the powder off was a little surprised at the amount I wanted; but I said that I might be absent many weeks in the mountains, and might want to drive a level in any lode that I might discover. I led him to believe that I had seen a spot in the mountains that gave good indications, and that two of my comrades were waiting there for my return to begin work at it. I sold the llamas to a man who carries goods from Ancon up to Canta, and got the same price that you gave for them."

Harry then told him the work on which he had been engaged since he had been away.

"Of course there is no hurry about the brackets, but as we could do nothing else without the powder and drills, it was just as well to get them out, as otherwise we might have been delayed when we had done our other work. We think that they weigh twenty pounds each, so that altogether they will be worth nearly four thousand pounds. Not a bad start. I am afraid we shan't make such quick work down below."

"We shall see," Dias said cheerfully, for now that his fear of the demons had passed he was as eager as Harry himself to begin the search for the treasure.

They discussed their plans for the next day. "I know nothing about blasting, señor. You give me instructions, and I will do my best to carry them out; but it is useless for me to talk of what I know nothing about."

"There is a lot of common sense in that, and yet in every work, Dias, sometimes while a skilled man is puzzling how to do a thing a looker-on will suggest a satisfactory plan. That treasure has been buried there I have no doubt whatever. They would never have gone to the labour of paving those cellars as carefully as they have done unless for some special purpose. The floor was undoubtedly made when the house was built, and if we find treasure-chambers there they will be those of the old people. Of course they may have been discovered by the Incas, and when they in turn wanted to bury treasure this place might occur to them as being particularly well fitted to escape search by Spaniards. However, to-morrow we shall learn something more about them. The first thing to do in the morning, when we have brought up the rest of the goods, is to sweep the floors of those chambers carefully. When we have done that we will determine where to set to work."

Two trips brought up the powder and instruments.

"We will take one of the kegs of powder down with us," said Harry, "and leave the other five in the empty room behind this. It is just as well not to have them in this room; the sparks fly about, and some things might catch fire. I don't think there is any real danger, but, at the same time, it is best to be on the safe side."

"There are a dozen pounds of candles in this bundle, señor. You did not tell me to get them, but I thought they might be useful."

"Thank you, Dias! they certainly will be useful. What are they?—tallow?"

"Yes, señor."

"Then before we go down we will get a couple of pieces of flat wood, and drive a peg into each, sharpened at the upper end. Candles stuck on these will stand upright, and we can put them down close to where we are working. They will give a better light than a torch, and leave us all free to use the tools. Did you think of buying some more tinder?"

"Yes, señor, I have five boxes, and half a dozen more flints."

They carried the keg of powder, the sledges, drills,

and wedges downstairs, and then Dias and José set to work to sweep out the two chambers. The work was easy, but they were obliged to stop several times, being almost choked with the light dust. Harry and Bertie offered to take their turn, but the others would not hear of it, and they were glad to go up to what they called their drawing-room until the work was done and the dust had settled a little. Then they examined the pavement carefully with their torches. They had hoped that they might find either copper rings, or at least holes where rings had been fastened, but there were no signs whatever of such things in either of the chambers.

"We will begin to work half-way down," Harry said. "Of course the treasure may lie near the cistern end, but the depth below the floor would be very shallow there. More likely the chambers would be at the deep end. If we begin in the middle we may be pretty sure that we have not passed them. We will begin rather nearer the passage wall than the other, as the depth there will be greater. It does not matter which stone we take, one is as likely as another. Step ten paces from the cistern, Bertie, and the stone you stop on we will try first."

When Bertie came to a standstill they carefully examined the pavement. "You are standing on one of the cracks, Bertie; I will stay there while you all bring the tools along."

"Shall I open the powder?" Bertie asked.

"No. It is no good doing that until we have quite decided what we are going to do. The wedges certainly won't go into this crack. I think our best plan will be to sink a bore-hole about two inches from the crack. We will drive it in in a slanting direction towards the edge, and in that way it will have more chance of blowing a piece out. First of all, we must make a slight indentation with a pick, otherwise we shan't get the bore to work. I will begin."

He took a pick and struck several blows.

"It is very hard stone," he said. "I have scarcely made a mark upon it."

He worked for some time, and then let Bertie take the pick. The lad struck a blow with all his strength, and then dropped the pick with a loud cry, wringing his hands as he did so.

"You have jarred your hands, Bertie; you should not hold the haft so tightly."

"It did sting!" Bertie said. "I feel as if I had taken hold of a red-hot poker. It has jarred my arm up to the shoulder; I can't go on at present."

"You try, Dias."

Dias went more carefully to work, knelt down on one knee, and proceeded to give a number of what seemed light blows.

"That is better than I did, Dias. The stone is crumbling into dust, and we shall be able to use the borer in a short time. Perhaps it will be better after all to drive the hole down straight. It will be easier to begin with; when we see how thick the stone is we shall know better how to proceed."

In ten minutes Dias had made a hole a quarter of an inch deep.

"Now, give me one of the borers—that one about two and a half feet long. I will hold it, and you strike to begin with Dias, only mind my fingers. Keep your eye fixed on top of the borer, and take one or two gentle strokes to begin with; then, when you know the distance you have to stand from it, do your best. You needn't really be afraid of striking my fingers. I shall hold the drill at least a foot from the top."

Dias began very carefully, gradually adding to the

strength of the blows as he got the right distance, and was soon striking hard. After each blow Harry turned the borer a slight distance round. When he heard the native's breath coming fast he told José to take a turn. The lad was nervous; the first blow he struck only grazed the top of the borer, and narrowly missed Harry's fingers. José dropped the sledge. "I can't do it, señor; I am afraid of hitting your fingers. I will sit down and hold it; it does not matter if you hit me."

"It would matter a good deal, José. No, no; you have got to learn."

"Would it not be well, señor," Dias said, "to take the borers and three hammers outside, and try them in soft ground? We could work them there till we all got accustomed always to hit them fair. There would be no occasion for them to be held, and we should get confident. I could have hit twice as hard as I did, if I hadn't been afraid of missing it."

"I think that is a very good plan, Dias. The loss of a day or two will make no difference. We shall make up for it afterwards."

Accordingly the drills and hammers were all taken up, and they were soon at work. Two or three gentle taps were given to the borers, to make them stand upright, and then all four began work. At first they often either missed the heads of the borers or struck them unevenly.

"It is well, Dias, that we carried out your suggestion, as I see I should have had an uncommonly good chance of getting my fingers smashed, or a wrist broken. I have missed as often as any of you."

They stopped frequently for breath, and at the end of an hour were glad to lay down their hammers. Dias was comparatively fresh; his practice as a woodsman now did him good service.

"I should have thought from the number of trees that

I have helped to cut down," Bertie said, "that I could hit pretty hard, but this is a great deal stiffer work. I should say that this hammer is at least twice the weight of the axe, and it is the lightest of the four. I ache a good deal worse than I did when I first chopped that tree down."

"So do I, Bertie. We will stick at this till we get accustomed to the work. By doing so we shall gain strength as well as skill."

"I will get some grease, señor, from Maria, and then I will rub your shoulders, and arms; that will do you a great deal of good."

"Thank you, Dias! It would be a good plan."

Dias did this to José as well as to the brothers, and then José in turn rubbed him.

They waited half an hour, and then Harry said: "Let us have another spell." This time a quarter of an hour sufficed. "It is of no use, Harry; I can't go on any longer Bertie said. "I feel as if my shoulders were broken."

"I am beginning to feel the same, Bertie. However, we are all hitting straighter now. We will go up into the shade and take it quietly for two or three hours; then we will have a spell again."

However, after the rest, they all agreed that it would be useless to try again, for they could not lift their arms over their heads without feeling acute pain. Three days were spent at this exercise, and at the end of that time they had gained confidence, and the heads of the drills were no longer missed.

After the first day they only worked for a quarter of an hour at a time, taking an hours rest. The pain in their arms had begun to abate. On the following day they practised striking alternately, three standing round one borer. They found this at first awkward, but by the end of the day they were able to strike in regular order, the blows falling faster after each other on to the drill.

"I think we shall do now," said Bertie. "No doubt we shall hit harder with a fortnight's practice, and shall be able to keep it up longer. However, I think that even now we have sufficient confidence in striking to be able to hold the borer without any fear of an accident."

The next day they began work early in the cellar. José volunteered to take the first turn to hold the drill.

"You understand, José, you must turn it round a little after each stroke, and in that way it will cut the hole regularly."

Harry took his place on one side of José, who sat with a leg on each side of the drill. Dias stood facing Harry, Bertie behind José, holding the torch so that its light fell strongly on the head of the drill. At first the two men struck gently, but gradually, as they grew confident, increased the weight of their strokes until they were hitting with their full power. After ten minutes they stopped. "Let us look at the hole," Harry said. "How far has it got down?"

José moved his position and Harry examined the hole. "About an eighth of an inch," he said. "Let us scrape the dust out of it."

"Shall we take a spell now, Harry?" Bertie said.

"No, we will wait five minutes and then go on again, and after that we will change places with you, relieving each other every twenty minutes."

The work went on, and at the end of two hours the hole was three inches deep. Another hour and a half and the drill suddenly went down.

"We are through it," Bertie said, "and I am not sorry."

"Now I will lift the drill up gently, Bertie; do you kneel down, and when I stop, take hold of it close to the floor, so that we may see the thickness of the stone."

"Five inches," he said as he measured it. "Now put on a little grease, Dias. I will lower it again, and we shall be perhaps able then to get some idea of what is underneath."

He lowered the drill and turned it round two or three times, and then carefully raised it. Some sand and little stones were sticking to it.

"Sand and gravel," he said. "That settles that point. Now we have done a good morning's work, and let us go up and have breakfast."

Maria looked enquiringly at them. "I was just coming down for you. Well, what have you done?"

"We have drilled one hole, Maria, and none of us have got our fingers smashed, so I think we have every reason to be satisfied with our first experience at the work."

As they breakfasted they talked matters over. Harry said he was certain that the thickness of the stone was not sufficient for them to break it up by blasting. "We shall have to try some other plan. It is equally certain that we cannot smash the stone with the sledge-hammers, and I don't think that the wedges would break it. Of course if we got one stone out it would be comparatively easy to lift the next, as we could put the crowbars under it. If we can do it no other way, we must drill a line of holes close to each other right across the stone, and we might then break off the piece between them and the crack and get our crowbars under the slab. It might be worth while to drill holes a foot apart, from the point where we have begun to the other end of the room. Of course of we found that gravel and stones were everywhere under the slabs we should learn nothing; but the opening to the chambers is probably covered by another stone, and if we found that, we could put in one or two more holes so as to be sure that it was flat, in which case we might smash it somehow. Of course, if we don't come upon a flat stone we shall conclude that they put a layer of sand and fine gravel over the slabs covering the vaults, and must then, as I say, get up one stone and gradually lift all the rest, clearing out the gravel as we go to the depth of a foot or so. In that way we shall make sure that we shall not miss any chamber there may be.

"I think that would certainly be the best plan. At present we are groping altogether in the dark, and it will take us a fortnight at least to make that row of holes close to each other, as you propose."

CHAPTER XIV

DISAPPOINTMENT

Six more days were spent in driving holes according to Harry's plan. The result was in all cases the same. Sand and small stones were brought up attached to the grease. They had now sunk the holes at a much more rapid rate than at first, for they were accustomed to the work, their muscles had hardened, and they were able to strike more frequently and with greater force. They would have got on still more quickly had it not been for the trouble in sharpening the drills. These were heated in the small blacksmith's fire Dias had brought. They were first placed in the fire, but this was not sufficiently hot to raise them beyond a dull red glow. When this was done a shovelful of glowing fragments was taken from the fire and placed on the hearth, and among these the small bellows raised the ends of the drills to a white heat, when of course they were easily worked. At first they had some difficulty in tempering them. Sometimes, when cooled, the points were too soft, at other times too brittle; but at the end of a week they had arrived at the proper medium. But one of the party had to work steadily to keep the drills in good order.

Just a fortnight after they had begun work they were about to begin a hole in a fresh stone. Talking it over, they had come to the conclusion that this was the most likely spot in the cellar for the situation of an underground chamber. Farther on there would scarce be width for one, for it was here but eight feet across. Where they had already tried there would scarcely have been depth enough. This seemed to be the happy medium.

Before setting to work Dias passed his torch over the stone. Presently he stopped. "Will you light two of the candles, señor; the torch flickers too much to see very plainly."

Somewhat surprised, for no such close examination had been made before, the candles were lighted and handed to him. Dias knelt down, and, with his face close to the stone, moved about carefully, examining it for some minutes without speaking.

"This stone, señor, is broken," he said at last, "broken into a dozen pieces, and they have been so carefully fitted together again that the dust that settled upon it quite prevented our seeing it till we swept it again just now, and it was only because there was a tiny chip out where I first looked that I noticed it."

Harry knelt down and also examined the stone. Like all the others, it had not been faced with tools. Consequently, although roughly even, there were slight irregularities in the surface. Now, as Dias pointed them out to him, he saw that there were lines running through it here and there.

"Look here, señor. The stone has been struck here. Here are some dents."

These were scarcely noticeable. The surface had taken the same colour as the rest of the stone. They were of irregular size, and from a quarter of an inch to an inch in diameter, and nearly in the centre of the stone, from which point several of the cracks started.

"It certainly looks as if the stone had been struck with something heavy," Harry said. "I should think, by the appearance, some very heavy piece of rock must have been dropped upon it."

"Yes, señor, very heavy rock—so heavy that there must have been many men to lift it."

"It must have been heavy indeed to break up this slab."

"Perhaps it is not so thick as the others," Dias suggested.

"I don't like it, Dias. Well, let us set to work. We will try the wedges there. They were no use against the solid stone, but they might move these pieces. Put one of the borers just at the place from which these cracks start—at least, I suppose they are cracks—and let us drive it in for an inch. You hold it, José. Don't turn it, we want it to go in just in a line with this crack. I know we cannot drive it in far, but at least we may make it go deep enough to give a wedge a hold in it."

Five such small holes were made in a crack that seemed to form a rough circle, then the wedges were put in, and they began to work with sledges. In ten minutes Harry, examining the place carefully, said: "The bit of stone is breaking up. There are lines running across it from the wedges. Give me the heaviest sledge." He swung it round his head and brought it down half a dozen times in the centre of the wedges. The cracks opened so far that he could see them without stooping.

"Now we will try with the crowbars," he said.

In ten minutes a fragment of the stone was got up; then they hammered on the wedges again, and a piece of rock, which was roughly seven or eight inches in diameter, broke completely off.

"It is only about two and a half inches thick," Harry said as he drew one of the fragments out. And, holding the candle to the hole, he went on: "And there is another slab underneath. That settles it. We are at the top of one of these vaults. The question is, is it empty? I am afraid it is. This stone has evidently been broken up and fitted in again with wonderful care."

"Why should it be fitted in carefully if they emptied the chamber?"

"That I can't tell you, Dias, and it is of no use trying to guess now. First of all, we will get the rest of the stone up. It won't be difficult, for now that we have made a start we can use our crowbars. José, run up and tell my brother to come down. We shall want him to help with the crowbar; and besides, he would of course, wish to be here, now that we on the point of making a discovery one way or the other."

In a minute Bertie came down with José, and Donna Maria followed. "José tells me you have broken a hole in one of the stones," Bertie exclaimed as he ran up.

"We have got a bit out of a broken stone, Bertie. This stone had been broken before, and evidently not by accident. It is only half the thickness of the others, and, as you can see, there is another slab underneath."

"Who can have broken it, Harry?"

"That question we cannot decide, but I should say probably the Incas. We agreed that it was very possible they discovered the hidden treasures of the Chimoos. They must have learned, as the Spaniards did, how cleverly these places were hidden, and it must have been as evident to them as it is to us, that if there was a hiding-place here, this must be the spot."

When one or two more pieces of the stone had been got out by the aid of the crowbars, the rest was removed without the least difficulty. Another slap two feet square was exposed. In the middle of this was a copper ring, and the slab fitted into a stone casing about eighteen inches wide. As soon as this casing was cleared, Dias and José took their places on one side, the two brothers on the other. A crowbar was thrust through the ring, and all of them, taking hold of the ends, lifted with all their strength. At first the stone did not move, but at the second effort it lifted suddenly. It was the same thickness as the one they had broken, and, on being moved, was easily handled. The torches were thrust down, and all peered eagerly into the vault. So far as they could see it was empty.

"Shall I jump down, señor?"

"No, the air may be bad, José. Run up and bring down a short length of rope, twenty feet will be ample. Now, let your torch drop down, Dias. If it burns, it will be safe for us to go down; if not, we must keep on dropping blazing brands into till they burn."

As, however, the torch burnt brightly, Harry lay down, and, saying, "Hold my legs, Bertie!" looked down into the vault. Eighteen inches below the surface, the hole widened out suddenly. A minute later Harry's head appeared above the surface again.

"It is empty," he said in as cheerful a voice as he could manage. "Of course it is a disappointment," he went on, "but I felt certain that it would be so directly we found the stone was cracked. The only hope was that the first finders of the treasure afterwards used the place for the same purpose. That they thought it possible they might do so is clear by the care with which they fitted the stones together."

None of the others spoke. The disappointment was a heavy one. Bertie broke the silence by saying: "Well, better luck next time. They may have found out this place, but there may be others which they did not find."

"Quite so, Bertie. Now we have got up one stone, it will be comparatively easy work getting up the others. We will take up every stone to the end, and then work back till we get to a place where there is not more than a couple of feet between the bottom of the stone and the top of the rock."

At this moment José ran into the room with the rope.

Harry took it, and dropped one end until it nearly touched the floor below. "Hold on," he said, "and I will slip down first." Half a minute later he stood at the bottom of the chamber, beside the torch which was still burning.

"It is only about three feet across at the bottom," he said; "the wall by the passage goes straight up, on the other side it is bare rock, so it is almost wedge-shaped. It is twenty feet long, and five high up to its roof, that makes it nearly seven to the upper part of the mouth." The vault was absolutely empty. He moved about for a minute then said: "Gold has been stored here. There are particles of gold at the bottom, and there is gold-dust in the cracks of the broken face of the rock. Now I will come up again. Hold the rope tight; I will climb about a yard then I can get my fingers on the ledge."

He was soon up. "Now, do any of you want to go down?" Dias and José shook their heads; and Bertie grumbled, "I don't want to look at the beastly hole; it has been trouble enough to get at it."

"Well, I think we will not do any more today, Dias. It has rather taken the heart out of one. Still, we could not expect to hit upon the treasure for the first time. We will go up and talk it over, and when we have smoked a pipe or two we shall be more inclined to take a cheerful view of the matter. We won't talk about it till we have got to the end of our second pipe."

The tobacco did its usual work, and it was with quite a cheerful voice that Bertie broke the silence: "The Incas must have been pretty sharp fellows to find that hole, Harry?"

"Well, very likely they heard that the Chimoos had treasure there. Indeed they must have known, because, you see, not one of the other stones is broken, so they evidently knew where that chamber was situated."

"Yes, I suppose that was it. Well, we are in fine working order now, and we shan't be very long getting the other stones up."

"Not very long this side anyhow, Bertie. We shall want some short blocks of wood to put under the stones as we raise them. I expect they are all five inches thick, and they must be a very big weight. Evidently it is going to be a longish job."

Another month passed in continuous labour. The stones had all been taken up in the basement they had first visited, but no other chamber had been found. The parallel chamber had given them much trouble at starting, as no stone had been found showing any cracks upon it, and they had had to blast one stone to pieces before they could begin to cut up the others. No chamber whatever had been discovered until they were within six feet of the farther end. Then one was found, but it showed no signs whatever of having ever been used.

"So far so bad," Harry said when the supper had been eaten almost in silence; "but that is no reason why we should be disheartened. If the Incas buried a treasure they may have thought it prudent to choose some other spot than that used by the old people."

"But where could it be, Harry? You agreed that there was not sufficient depth between the floors for any place of concealment."

"That is so, Bertie, of course. I have been thinking of it a lot during the past few days, when the chances of our finding a treasure under the basement were nearly extinguished. There are still the side walls."

"The side walls!" Bertie repeated. "Surely they are built against the rock?"

"Yes, but we don't know how straight the wall of rock is. You see, they did not build against it at all in the basement, but above that the side walls begin. The rock must have been irregular, and as the walls were built the space behind may have been filled in or may not. When they came to build they may have found that there was a cavern or caverns in the rock—nothing is more likely —and they may have left some sort of entrance to these caverns, either as a place of refuge to the garrison if the place were taken, or as a hiding-place. They might have thought it more secure for this purpose than the underground chamber, which was their general hiding-place. At any rate it is possible, and to-morrow I vote that we have a thorough inspection of the walls of the storeroom below this. That would be the most likely place, for near the sea-level the chances of finding caverns would be much greater than higher up."

Bertie's face brightened as Harry proceeded.

"It certainly seems possible, Harry. Of course the other place seemed so much more likely to us that we have never given the side walls a thought. We may find something there after all. I do hope we may, old boy. I cannot believe that after things have gone altogether so well with us, and we have been twice so near finding treasure, that we should fail after all. Which side shall we begin on?"

"We will have a look at them before we decide, Bertie. We have not really examined them since the first day; I really forget what stores we found in the two siderooms."

An examination in the morning showed that the passage near the entrance to the rock on the left-hand side had been used for fuel, that on the other side was filled at the upper end with skins for some distance, and spears and sheaves of arrows were piled against the outer wall along the rest of the distance.

"Which do you think is the most likely hiding-place?"

"I should say the right-hand passage. The other with

the firewood in it might be visited every day, but the spears and arrows would only be wanted in case of any attacks upon the castle, or to arm a large force going out to give battle there. They would naturally put anything they wanted to hide in the passage less likely to be visited."

"That does seem probable," Bertie agreed; "therefore, hurrah for the right-hand side!"

"I still think, señor," Dias said, "that there must be treasure concealed somewhere. I should not think a guard would have been placed here, and remained here so many years still keeping watch, as we find they did at that big loophole on the top floor, unless there was something to watch."

"Quite so, Dias. I have thought that over in every way, and I can see no possible motive for their being here except to prevent the place from being examined. That was needless if there was nothing to guard, and nothing to take away, except those silver brackets, which in those days would scarcely have been worth the trouble of getting out and carrying away. There must be treasure somewhere. We know now that it is not in the basement, and we will try these side walls, even if we have to blow half of them in; there is no doubt that the stones are at least as thick as those at the end, but they will not be difficult to manage. I noticed in the upper story that they had not taken the trouble to fit them nearly so accurately as they did those of the outer walls. I don't say that they didn't fit well, but the stones were of irregular sizes, and I have no doubt that in many places we could prise them out with a crowbar. Once an opening is made, there will be no difficulty in getting a lot of them out, as the old people did not use cement or mortar. Well, to-morrow morning we will move all the spears and arrows across to the other side of that passage and have a good look at the stones, but we will go up first and look at the side walls of all the other rooms and see if they are of the same build. There may be some difference which we have not noticed. You see all the side walls of this room are built like those in front. I didn't notice whether it was the same in the other rooms."

"I will look at once," Dias said, lighting a torch at the fire.

"No, señor," he said, when in ten minutes he returned; "none of the walls on this floor are built of stone like this. This was the grand chamber, the stones are all nearly one size, and so well fitted that you can hardly see where they join each other. In the other rooms they are not so, but the stones are, as you noticed above, irregular in size, and although they fit closely, there is no attempt to conceal the cracks."

"Thank you, Dias! Well, we won't look any more to-night; we shall see in the morning if the room below us is built in the same way. At any rate we have done enough for today."

They were up a daybreak, and after taking their usual cup of coffee lit the torches and descended the stairs to the floor below.

As soon as they reached the right-hand wall, Harry exclaimed: "This is built in the same way as the one we have left! The stones are squared and fitted together as closely as those in the drawing-room. Then why should that be, except in that one room? The side walls all the way up are roughly built. Why should they have taken the trouble on this floor to build these, which are only meant as store-rooms, when even in the rooms above, which were meant for habitation of the chief and his family, the rough work was deemed sufficiently good? There must have been some motive for this Dias."

"There must have been, señor; it is certainly strange."

"First of all, let us clear the wall and take a general view of it. Guessing won't help us; but I have the strongest hopes that behind one of these stones lies a cavern. By the way, Dias, take a torch and go into the next chamber and see if the stones are solid there."

"They are just the same as those here," Dias said when he returned.

"I would rather that it had been the other way," Harry said, "for then I should have been more sure that there was some special reason for their building them in this way here."

It took them all half an hour's work to move the spears and arrows to the other side.

"Do you think, Harry, if we were to tap the stones we should be able to find whether there is a hollow behind any of them?"

Harry shook his head.

"Not in the least. I have no doubt these stones are two or three feet thick, and there could be no difference in the sound they would make if struck, whether they were filled in solid behind or had no backing. To begin with, we will make a careful examination of the walls. Possibly we shall see some signs of a stone having been moved. It would be very much more difficult to take one of the great blocks out and put it in again than it would be to get up one of the paving-stones."

When they had gone about half-way along, examining each stone with the greatest care, Bertie, who was ahead of the rest, and passing the candle along the edge of every joint, said, "Look here! this stone projects nearly half an inch beyond the rest."

The others gathered round him. The stone was of unusual size, being fully two and a half feet wide and four feet long, the bottom joint being two feet above the floor.

Bertie moved along to let others look at the edge. He was keeping his finger on the joint, and they had scarcely come up when he said, "The other end of the stone is sunk in about as much as this end projects."

"Something certainly occured to shift this stone a little," Harry said, examining it carefully. "It is curious. If others had been displaced, one would have put it down to the shock of an earthquake—a common enough occurrence here—but both above and below it the stones are level with the others, and nowhere about the house have we seen such another displacement. Look! there is a heap of rubbish along the foot of the wall here. Stir it up, Dias, and let us see what it is."

"It is sand and small stones, and some chips that look like chips of rock."

"Yes, these bits look, as you say, as if they had been chipped off a rock, not like water-worn stones. Though how they got here, where everywhere else things are perfectly tidy, I cannot say. However, we can think that over afterwards. Now for the stone! Let us all put our weight against this projecting end. I don't in the least expect that we can move it, but at any rate we can try."

They all pushed together.

"I think it moved a little," Harry said, and looked at the edge.

"Yes, it is not above half as far out now as it was."

"That is curious, for if it is as thick as we took it to be, it would weigh at least a couple of tons. We won't try to push it any farther. I am sorry we pushed it at all. Now, give me that heavy sledge, José, possibly there may be a hollow sound to it. I will hit at the other end, for I don't want this to go in any farther."

He went to the stone beyond it first and struck two or three blows with all his strength. Then he did the same with the stone that they were examining.

"I don't think it gives such a dead sound," he said.

The others were all of the same opinion.

"Good! This is another piece of luck," he said. "We have certainly hit on something out of the way."

"Your hammering has brought this end out again, Harry," Bertie said.

"So it has, and it has pushed this end in a little. Let us try again." But although all took turns with the sledges, they could make no further impression on the stone.

"Well, we will try the drills," Harry said. "In the first place, we will find out how thick it is."

They at once set to work with the drill. Progress was slower than it had been before, because, instead of striking down on the head of thed rill, they had now to swing the hammer sideways and lost the advantage of its weight; and they were obliged to work very carefully, as a miss would have seriously damaged the one holding the drill. It took them four hours' steady work to get the hole in three inches. Ten minutes later, to their astonishment, the drill suddenly disappeared. Dias, who was striking, nearly fell, for instead of the resistance he had expected, the drill shot forward; the hammer hit José, who had this time been holding the drill, a heavy blow on the arm, causing him to utter a shout of pain.

Harry, who was sitting down having breakfast, having just handed his hammer to Bertie, jumped to his feet.

"How did you manage that, Dias? I suppose it slipped off the head. You must have hit José a very heavy blow."

"I have hit him a heavy blow, señor, and nearly tumbled down myself; but I struck the drill fairly enough, and it has gone."

"Gone where, Dias?"

"I think it must have gone right through the hole, señor."

"Then there is an empty space behind!" Harry

shouted joyfully. "However," he went on in changed tones, "we must see to José first. That blow may have fractured his arm. Let me look, José. No, I don't think anything is broken, but there is a nasty cut on the wrist. It is fortunate that you were not striking straight down, Dias, for I am sure we have not put anything approaching the strength into our blows, now we are hitting sideways, that we exerted before. You had better go up to Maria, José, and get her to bathe your wrist with cold water, and put on a bandage."

"Now, señor, what shall we do next?"

"Well, now that we know that its weight cannot be anything very great, and that certainly to some extent it can be moved, we will try hammering again at that end. Do you stand three or four feet beyond it, so as to be able to bring your sledge down with all your strength just on the lower corner. I will face you and strike six or eight inches above where you hit. Of course we must both bring our hammers down at the same instant. We shall be able to do that after two or three trials. Stand at the other end of the stone, Bertie, and tell us if it moves at all."

After one or two attempts the two men got to swing their hammers so as to strike precisely at the same moment, and when half a dozen blows had fallen, Bertie said: "It comes out a little at each blow. It is not much, but it comes."

Three or four minutes later he reported, "It is an inch and a half out now, and there is room to get the end of a crowbar in here."

"That is curious," Harry said as he lowered his sledge-hammer, and, taking up the candle, examined the end where he had been striking.

"This is sunk about the same distance, Bertie. The stone must work somehow on a pivot."

They now put a crowbar into the end Bertie had been watching, and all three threw their weight on the lever. Slowly the stone yielded to the pressure, and moved farther and farther out. It was pushed open until the crowbar could act no longer as a lever, but they could now get a hold of the inside edge. It was only very slowly and with repeated efforts that they could turn the stone round, and at last it stood fairly at right angles to the wall, dividing the opening into equal parts about two feet four each.

"There is a pivot under it; that is quite evident. It may be a copper ball in the stone below, or it may be that a knob of the upper stone projects into a hole in the lower. However, it does not matter how it works. Here is an opening into something. Dias, will you go upstairs and tell your wife and José to come down? They had better bring half a dozen more torches. Our stock here is getting low, and we shall want as much light as possible. It is only fair that we should all share in the discovery."

Dias went off.

"Now, Bertie, we must not let our hopes grow too high. I think it is more likely than not that we shall find nothing here."

"Why do you think so, Harry? I made sure we had as good as got the treasure."

"I think, if there had been treasure," Harry went on, "that this stone would have been closed with the greatest care. They would hardly have left it so carelessly closed that anyone who examined the wall would have noticed it, just as we did. We found the other places most carefully closed, though there was nothing in them."

"Perhaps there was something that prevented them from shutting—a little stone or something."

"But we know that that wasn't so, Bertie, because the

stone yielded to our weight; and if it did so now, it could have been shut with greatest ease originally, when no doubt the pivot was kept oiled, and the whole worked perfectly smoothly. It is almost certain that they were able in some way to fasten it securely when it was shut. What is that piece of square stone lying there?"

"It fell down from above just as the slab opened."

Harry took it up. It was about six inches long by two inches square.

"It is a very hard stone," he said—"granite, I should say. I expect you will find that it fits into a hole in the stone above."

"Yes, there is a hole here," Bertie said, feeling it; "the stone goes right in."

"Well, I think Bertie, you will find a hole in that end of the stone we moved that it will fit."

Bertie crept in, and felt along the top of the stone.

"Yes, there is a hole here about the same size as the stone, but it is not more than three inches deep."

"Then, that stone was the bolt, Bertie. You see it was pushed up, and the door then closed; and when the stone was exactly in its place, it would drop into the hole and keep it from moving, and nothing short of breaking up the bolt would give an entrance. It is lucky that we did not push it quite to; another quarter of an inch and that bolt would have fallen, and we could not have moved it unless by smashing the whole thing into bits. That was why they did not quite close the stone; they wanted to get in again."

"Here come the others!"

Maria had been washing some clothes in the stream, and they had therefore been longer in coming than if she had been in the room. They all looked greatly excited.

"So you have found it, señor!" Dias exclaimed in delight.

"We have found an entrance into somewhere, but I am afraid it will be as empty as the other chambers."

"Why do you think so, señor?" Dias asked in dismay.

Harry repeated the reasons he had given Bertie for belief that the stone must have been left in such a position as to be easily opened when required.

"Why should it have been left so?"

"Because the treasure they had expected had never arrived. It is possible that when the Incas discovered the treasure in that chamber we searched, they may also have found this entrance. It may have been shown to them by one of the prisoners, and they may have broken the stone here into pieces as they broke that over the chamber afterwards. Seeing what a splendid hiding-place it was, they may have, when the Spaniards first arrived, made another stone to fit, with the intention of using it for a hiding-place themselves. The fact that the stone was left so that it could be at once opened is conclusive proof to my mind that the treasure never came. That heap of sand, small stones, and chips of rock is another proof that they were ready to receive treasure, and it was probably swept out of the chamber that is behind here, and would, of course, have been removed when the treasure was put in and the door closed; but as the treasure never did come, it was left where it lay. However, we will now go and see. I have only kept you waiting because I did not want you to be disappointed."

One by one they crept through the opening. For four feet in, the passage was the same width as the stone, but two feet deeper; then it at once opened into a large cavern.

"This wall was four feet thick, you see, Dias. Apparently squared stone was only used for the facing, as the stones are of irregular shape on the back. This would be a natural cavern, and a splendid hiding-place it makes. No doubt its existence was one of the reasons for building this castle."

The cavern was some twelve feet wide, and thirty feet high at the mouth; the floor sloped up sharply, and the sides contracted, and met forty feet from the mouth. The floor had been cut into steps two feet wide running across the cave and extending to the back. These steps were faced with a perfectly flat slab of stone. The cave was empty.

The natives uttered loud exclamations of disappointment and regret.

Harry had so thoroughly made up his mind that nothing would be found there that he surveyed the place calmly and in silence. Bertie imitated his example with some difficulty, for he too was bitterly disappointed.

"You see, Dias," Harry went on quietly, "this place was prepared to receive treasure. The steps have all been swept perfectly clean. You see, the gold could be piled up, and no doubt the steps were cut and faced with stone to prevent any gold dust that might fall from the bags, in which, no doubt, it would be brought, and small nuggets, from falling into the cracks and crevices of the rock. I should say that in all probability they expected that treasure ship that was lost, and had everything in readiness for hiding the cargo here directly it came. It never did come. The door was shut as far as it could be without the bolt falling down and fastening it; then they waited for the ship; and if it did not arrive, other treasure might be brought by land. Well, it cannot be helped. So far we have failed. There may still be treasure hidden somewhere. We cannot say that we have searched the place thoroughly yet."

For another six weeks they worked hard. The wall was

broken through in several places, but no signs of the existence of any other cavern or hiding-place was discovered.

"I should give it up," Harry said, when at the end of that time they were sitting gloomily round the fire, "but for one thing: I can see no possible explanation why a party of men should have been left here, and a guard kept, for perhaps a hundred years, perhaps more, and the stories about demons been circulated, and people who ventured to approach been murdered, unless there had been some good reason for it. That reason could only have been, as far as I can see, that there was a treasure hidden here. I have turned it over and over in my mind a thousand times, and I can think of no other reason. Can you, Bertie, or you, Dias?"

"No," Bertie replied. "I have often thought about it; but, as you say, there must have been some good reason, for no people in their senses would have spent their lives in this old place, and starved here, unless they had some cause for it."

Dias made no reply beyond shaking his head.

"You see," Harry went on, "they kept up their watch to the end. There were those two skeletons of men who had died at their post at that curious window where nothing could be seen. I hate to give up the search, and yet we seem to have tried every point where there was a possibility of a hiding-place existing."

CHAPTER XV

THE TREASURE

THE next morning Harry said:

"I will go upstairs to that look-out place again. I have been up there pretty nearly every day, and stared down. I can't get it out of my mind that the key of the mystery lies there, and that that hole was made for some other purpose than merely throwing stones out on to any of those who might go in behind the rocks. I have puzzled and worried over it."

"Shall I come up with you, Harry?"

"No, I would rather you didn't. I will go up by myself and spend the morning there; some idea may occur to me. You may as well all have a quiet day of it."

He lit his pipe and went upstairs. José went off to the mules, and Bertie descended the ladder, and strolled round what they called the courtyard, looking for eggs among the rocks and in the tufts of grass growing higher up. Dias scattered a few handfuls of maize to the chickens and then assisted Maria to catch two of them; after which he descended the ladder and sat down gloomily upon a stone. He had become more and more depressed in spirits as the search became daily more hopeless; and although he worked as hard as anyone, he seldom spoke, while Harry and his brother often joked, and showed no outward signs of disappointment. An hour passed, and then Harry appeared suddenly at the window.

"Bertie, Dias, come up at once, I have an idea!"

They ran to the ladder and climbed up. The excitement with which he spoke showed that the idea was an important one. "Now, Dias," he broke out as they joined him, "we know, don't we, that a part of the Incas' treasure was sent off by boat, and the belief of the Indians was that it was never heard of again."

"That is so, señor. There was certainly a storm the day after it started, and, as I have told you, it was never heard of again. Had it been, a report of it would surely have come down."

"I believe, Dias, that the boat was dashed to pieces against that line of rocks outside the entrance to the passage. We have reason to believe that the people here were expecting the treasure to arrive, and had the entrance to the cave in readiness to receive it. Certainly no better place could have been chosen for concealment. The boat may have been coming here when the storm broke and drove them towards the shore. They probably attempted to gain the mouth of the cove, but missed it, and were dashed to pieces against the rocks. The Indians on guard here no doubt saw it, and would be sure that the heavy sacks or boxes containing the gold would sink to the bottom. They would lie perfectly secure there, even more secure than if they had been removed and placed in the cave, and could always be recovered when the Spaniards left, so they were content to leave them there. Still, they obeyed the orders they had received to keep watch for ever over the treasure, and to do so knocked that strange hole through the wall and always kept two men on guard there.

"So it must have gone on. They and those who succeeded them never wavered. Doubtless they received food from their friends outside, or some of them went out, as you have done, to fetch it in. Then came a time when, for some reason or other—doubtless, as I supposed before, when the Spaniards swept pretty nearly all the natives up to work in the mines, and they themselves dared not issue out—the attempt to get food was made, when too late, by the men whose skeletons we found on the steps when we first came here; and the rest were all too feeble to repeat the experiment, and died—the two sentinels at their post, the rest in the room where we found them."

"Hurrah!" Bertie shouted, "I have no doubt you have hit it, Harry. Shall we go and have a trial at once?"

"What do you think, Dias?" Harry said.

"I think it is quite possible, señor. Certainly, if the Indians had been told to guard the treasure, they would do so always. You know how they kept the secrets entrusted to them whatever tortures they were put to. If the gold had been, as you say, lost among the rocks, I do think they would have still watched the place. I thought it strange that they should have made that hole, but when you said that they might have made it to throw stones down it seemed to me to be likely enough; but the other suggestion is more probable. Well, señor, I am ready to try it, but I am not a very good swimmer."

"My brother and I are both good swimmers, and we will do that part of the work. The hardest part will be getting it up, and you will be able to give us your help at that."

"Well, let us be off," Bertie said; "I am all on thorns to begin. We shall soon find it out. If it is there, it is almost certain to be at the foot of the rocks, though, of course, it is possible that the boat sank before striking them. At any rate, I feel sure she went down somewhere within the area that can be seen through that hole. It won't take many day's diving to search every yard of the bottom."

They hastily descended the ladder, and, divesting themselves of their clothes, swam out through the opening. Dias climbed up on the rocks, the others swam round by the ends of the barrier. The water was so warm that they would be able to remain in it for any time without inconvenience.

"We need not begin here, Bertie; we are outside the line of sight. From that hole I could not see the end of these rocks. We will start at the middle, and work in opposite directions."

On arriving off the centre of the wall both dived. The depth was about twelve feet, and as the water was perfectly clear, Harry could see four or five feet round him. He was obliged to swim carefully, for the bottom was covered with rocks, for the most part rounded by the action of the sea. For an hour he continued his search, by which time he had reached nearly the end of the line of rocks. Then he landed on a ledge of rock and sat down, calling to Bertie to join him.

"We will rest for a quarter of an hour," he said, "and then begin again. This time we will keep twenty or thirty feet farther out; it is more likely to be there than close in. If the boat struck, the next wave would sweep over her, and she would probably go down stern first, and her cargo would fall out that way."

After their rest they started again, swam out a few strokes, and then dived. Harry had gone down five or six times, when, on his coming to the surface, he heard a shout, and saw Bertie swimming towards him.

"I have found them, Harry! There are a number of ingots, but they were so heavy that I could not bring one of them to the surface."

As Harry reached him the lad turned round and swam back. "There they are, just opposite that cleft in the rock! I looked directly I came up so as to know the exact spot."

Harry trod water for half a minute, then took a long breath and dived.

It was as Bertie had said. Scattered among the rocks were a score of ingots. They had lost their brilliancy, but shone with a dull copperish hue, with bright gleams here and there where rocks had grated against them. Putting one hand on a block of rock he lifted one of them with the other.

"About twenty pounds," he said to himself. "Thank God, Hilda is as good as won!" Then he rose to the surface. "Shake hands, Bertie; there is enough there to make us all rich for life. Now we will get back again. We have to think matters over, and see how they are to be got ashore. There is no hurry; they have lain there for three hundred years, and would lie there as much longer if we did not take them. We have found them, Dias!" he shouted; and the latter gave a yell of delight. "Swim ashore, and we will join you there."

Not another word was spoken until they had dressed and walked out.

"I am too excited even to think," Harry broke out. "It is time for dinner. When we have had that and smoked a pipe I shall be able to talk calmly over it."

Maria was wild with delight at the news, and laughed and cried by turns. Even José, who was accustomed to take all things quietly, was almost as excited. The woman was only called to herself when Harry said, laughing, "Maria, for the first time since we started from Lima, you are letting the dinner burn."

"To think of it!" she cried. "It is your fault, señor; you should not have told me about it till we sat down."

"You won't have to cook much longer, Maria. You will be able now to have a servant, and a house as big as you like, and a beautiful garden."

"I should not like that, señor; what should I do all day with myself?"

"I am glad, señor, glad for your sake," Dias said

gravely. "To us it will make no difference. You said there was enough there to make us rich. Assuredly that is so; but not one peso of it will we touch. No man with Indian blood in his veins, not even the poorest in Peru, would have aught to do with an ounce of the Incas' treasures. When they were buried, a curse was laid upon any who betrayed their hiding-place or who ever touched the gold."

"Well, Dias, I will not try to persuade you; but I have money of my own, and from that I will give you enough to make you comfortable for life, and that you can take without feeling that you have incurred any curse from the finding of this treasure."

"I thank you heartily," Dias said gratefully; "I thank you with all my heart. I have ever been a wanderer, and now I will gladly settle down. I do not desire wealth, but enough to live on in comfort with my wife, and only to travel when it pleases me."

"You shall have enough for that and more, Dias."

After some more meat had been cooked and eaten, and he had smoked a pipe, Harry said: "A boat would, of course, be the best thing, but there are difficulties connected with it. There is no spot, as far as I know, where we could land for fifteen miles on either side, and there would only be small villages where everything we did would be seen and talked about. There is no place where we could keep a boat here, for if even a slight breeze sprang up the swell coming in round the passage between the rocks and the cliff would smash her up in no time."

"That is so, señor."

Harry was silent again for some time, and then said: "The only plan I can think of is to get some strong leather bags. Then we could take one down with us when we dive, with a strong cord tied to it, put a couple of the ingots into it, and you could haul it up on to the rocks, and so on until we have finished a day's work. Then we could carry them to this side of the rocks; there you could put them, three or four at a time, into the bag, and drop them down in the water. We would swim up the tunnel and haul them in, and then bring the bag back again. We shan't be able to get anything approaching all the ingots, for a great many of them must have gone in between the crevices of the rocks, and unless we broke it up with powder, which would be next to impossible without a diving-dress and air-pumps and all sorts of things, which cannot be bought in this country, we could not get at them. However, we have only just begun to look for them yet; we may come across a pile. Heavy as the sea must be on this coast in a gale, I hardly think it would much affect a pile of ingots; their weight would keep them steady even were big rocks rolled about.

"I think the best thing, Dias, would be for you to go off with two or three mules. We shall soon be running short of provisions, and you had better get enough flour and dried meat to last us for a month. I don't suppose we shall be as long as that, but it is as well to have a good store so as not to have to make the journey again. Then you had better get twenty leather bags, such as those in which they bring the ore down from the mountains. We have plenty of stout rope, but we shall want some thin cord for tying the necks of the bags. You may as well bring another keg of spirits, brandy if you can get it, a bag of coffee, and some sugar, and anything else you can think of. Now I am a millionaire we can afford to be comfortable. By the way, we might as well this afternoon get the rest of those silver brackets out. These are not part of the Incas' treasure, and you can take them as your share without fear of the curse. It would be best for you to smelt them down; I know all of you natives can do that."

"But it is altogether too much, señor; it is noble of you to offer it me."

"Not at all; we owe everything we find to you, and it would be only fair that you should have at least a third of the gold. But still, if you won't touch that, you must take the silver."

"But I heard you say that it was worth four thousand pounds."

"Well, if we are lucky we shall get twenty times as much, Dias."

"Certainly we will take it, señor, and grateful we shall both be to you," Maria said: "and so will José, who will inherit it all some day, as he is the only relative we have."

"You had better buy some bags of charcoal, Dias. I suppose you will use that small hearth we have?"

"No, señor, it would take an immense time to do it in that. I will load one of the mules with hard bricks."

"You will want two mules to carry a hundred, Dias— I think they weigh about four pounds and a half each. Will that be enough?"

"Plenty, señor; but I shall want another bellows. José and I can work the two of them, and that will make a great heat. We can melt two or three hundred pounds a day. I have helped to make many a furnace up in the mountains, and I know very well all about the way to build and work them."

"Very well, then, that is settled. You had better start tomorrow morning with José, and we will spend the day in finding out a litle more about the gold."

Dias started the next morning, and the two brothers were in the water most of the day. Harry found, as he had expected, that a great deal of the treasure had sunk out of reach between the rocks; but he came upon one pile, which had apparently been originally packed packed in sacks or skins, lying in a heap a little farther out than they had before searched. He had no doubt that this was the point where the stern of the boat had sunk, and a considerable portion of the contents had been shot out, while the rest had been scattered about as the boat broke up, and as the skins rotted their contents had fallen between the rocks. There were, as nearly as he could calculate, two hundred and fifty to three hundred ingots in the pile.

"I need not trouble about the rest," he laughed to himself. "Each ingot, if it weighs twenty pounds, is worth a thousand. Two hundred of them would make me as rich as any man can want to be. I can hardly believe in my luck; it is stupendous. Fancy a half-pay lieutenant with two hundred thousand pounds! Old Fortescue will become one of the most complaisant of fathers-in-law.

The evening before Dias left, Harry had written a letter for him to post at Callao, telling Hilda to keep up a brave heart, for that he hoped to be at home before the end of the second year with money enough to satisfy her father.

"I should not tell you so unless I felt certain of what I am saying. I told you before I left that it was almost a forlorn hope that I was undertaking, and that the chances were ten thousand to one against me. I think now that the one chance has turned up, and I hope to be home within two months of the time that you receive this letter."

When Dias returned after two day's absence the work began. Each morning they worked together to bring up the gold and piling the ingots on the rock. It was slower work than Harry had expected, for on hauling the bag to the rocks it was often caught by the boulders, and he and Bertie sometimes had to dive four or five times before they could free it and get it ashore. The gold was piled in the tunnel just beyond the water. In a fortnight the last ingot they could get at was stored with its fellows —two hundred and eighty-two in all.

They had repeatedly talked over the best plan of getting the gold away, and finally concluded that it would be risking too much to take into a town, and that the best plan would be for Harry to buy a boat at Callao, which, as a naval officer, would be natural enough. They decided to procure three times as many bags as the ingots would really require, and that they should put in each bag three ingots only, filling it up with pieces of stone, so that the weight should not exceed what it would have been were the contents heavy ore. Harry arranged that he would go down to Callao, buy a large boat, and after having made several excursions, to accustom the officials at Callao to seeing him going about, he would make a bargain with the captains of two ships about to sail to England, to carry about two tons each of ore, which he could put on board them after dark, so as to avoid the extortion he would have to submit to before the port officials and others would allow him to ship it. The question that puzzled them most was the best way of taking the bags into the boat. Dias was in favour of their being carried on the mules to a point lower down the coast, at which they could be loaded into the boat.

"It would be only necessary to carry the gold," he said, "the stones to fill the bags could be put in there."

The objection to this was that they might be observed a work, and that at most points it would be difficult both to run the boat up and to get her off again through the rollers. If the boat were brought round into the inlet she could be loaded there comfortably. The only fear was of being caught in a gale. But as gales were by no means frequent the risk was small; and should a sudden storm come on when she was lying there, and she was broken up, it would be easy to recover the gold from the shallow water behind the rocks. This was therefore settled. Only half the treasure was to be taken away at once, and not till this had been got on board a ship and the vessel had sailed would the boat come back for the rest of their treasure.

Dias was at once to start with the mules and carry the silver, in two journeys, to a safe place among the mountains. There he could bury it in three or four hiding-places, to be fetched out as he might require it, only taking some fifty pounds to Lima. Here he was to dispose of a portion of it to one of the dealers who made it his business to buy up silver from the natives. As many of these worked small mines, and sent down the produce once a month to Lima, there would be nothing suspicious in its being offered for sale, especially as it would be known that Dias had been away for a very long time among the mountains. It was necessary that the sale should be effected at once, because Harry's stock of money was running very low, and he would have to pay for the passage of Bertie and himself to England, and for the freight of the gold. Dias was to dispose later on of all the remaining stores, the powder and tools, and the three riding mules.

Two days later the last of the silver brackets had been melted, and Dias and Harry started with the eight mules, six of them being laden with the silver. They struck back at once into the hills, and after travelling for two days, ascended a wild gorge. "It is not once a year that anyone would come up here, señor. There is no way out of it. We can bury the silver here with a certainty that it will be safe from disturbance."

"Yes, it will be safe here; and as you want it you have only to make a journey with a couple of mules to fetch as much as you require, carry it home, and bury it in your garden or under the house; then you could from time to time take a few ingots into the town and dispose of them. But to begin with, I will borrow fifty pounds weight of it, and get you to dispose of it for me at Lima. My money is beginning to run short. I shall have to pay for the freight of the gold and my own passage home, and to buy a boat large enough to carry half the treasure. It is not likely that there will be two vessels sailing at the same time, in which case I shall make two trips. As I should not put it on board until the night before the ship sailed, of course I could go home with the second lot."

"I shall never know what to do with a tenth part of this silver, señor. It would never do for me to make a show of being rich; the authorities would seize me, and perhaps torture me to make me reveal the source of my wealth."

"Well, there are thousands of your countrymen in the deepest poverty, Dias; you could secretly help those in distress; a single ingot, ten pounds in weight, would be a fortune to them. And when you die you might get a respectable lawyer to make out a will, leaving your treasure to some charity for the benefit of Indians, giving, of course, instructions where the treasure is to be found."

"That is good," Dias said. "Thank you, señor! that will make me very happy."

They had brought a pick and shovel with them, and, dividing the bags, buried them at some distance apart, rolling stones to cover up the hiding-places, and obliterating any signs of the ground having been disturbed. A hundred pounds were left out, and with this in their saddle-bags they arrived at Lima two days later.

Harry went on alone into Callao. He had no difficulty in purchasing a ship's boat in fair condition. She carried two lug-sails, and was amply large enough for the purpose for which she was required, being nearly thirty feet long with a beam of six feet. He got her cheaply, for the ship to which she belonged had been wrecked some distance along the coast, and a portion of the crew had launched her and made their way to Callao; the mate, who was the sole surviving officer, was glad to accept the ten pounds Harry offered for her, as this would enable the crew to exist until they could obtain a passage home, or ship on board some British vessel short of hands. The boat was too large to be worked by one man, and seeing that the mate was an honest and intelligent fellow, Harry arranged with him to aid him to sail the boat, and each day they went out for some hours. After spending a week in apparent idleness, and getting to know more of the man, Harry told him that he had really bought the boat for the purpose of getting some ore he had discovered on board a ship homeward-bound.

"You know what these Peruvians are," he said, "and how jealous they are of our getting hold of mines, so I have got to do the thing quietly, and the only way will be to take the ore off by night. It is on a spot some eighty miles along the coast. I am going off tomorow to get it ready for embarkation, and I shall be away about a week. I find that the *London* will leave in ten days, and I shall get it put on board the night before she sails. While I am away, look after the boat. The *Nancy* will sail five days later. I am going to put half on board each ship, as I am anxious to ensure that some at least of the ore shall reach home, so as to be analysed, and see if it is as rich as I hope. But be sure not to mention a word of this to a soul. I should have immense trouble with the authorities if it got about that I had discovered a mine."

"I understand, sir. You may be quite sure I shall say nothing about it."

"How are your men getting on?"

"Four are shipped on board the *Esmeralda,* which sailed yesterday, the others are hanging on till they can get berths. I hope a few will be able to go in the two ships you name, but they haven't applied at present. Some of the crew may desert before the time for sailing comes, and of course they would get better paid if they went as part of the crew than if they merely worked their passage home."

"I am sorry for them," Harry said. "Here is another five pounds to help them to hold on. As an old naval officer I can feel for men in such a place."

Dias, after selling the silver, had, a week before, returned with the mules to the castle, and on his arrival there had sent José to join Harry and bring news to them of the day on which the boat would arrive. Dias and Bertie were packing half the bags, of which the former took with him an ample supply, to get the gold out on the rocks facing the entrance, so that they could be shipped without delay. Great pains were taken in packing the bags so that the three ingots placed in each should be completely surrounded by stones. Anyone who might take a fancy to feel them, in order to ascertain their contents, would have no reason to suppose that they carried anything beyond the ore they were stated to contain.

Harry had no difficulty in arranging with the captain of the *London* to take from a ton and a half to two tons of ore the night before he sailed, and three days before this Harry started with the mate. There was but a light breeze, and it was daylight next morning before they arrived. A pole had been stuck up at the edge of the cliff just above the cavern, and as it became dark a lantern was also placed there, so they had no trouble in finding the entrance of the little cove.

"It is a rum-looking place, sir," the man said. "As far as I can see there is no break in the cliffs."

"It is a curious place, but you will find the bags with the ore on the rocks inside here ready for us, and my brother and one of my men waiting there. They will have made us out an hour ago, so we can load up at once and get out of this tiny creek. I don't want to stay in there any longer than is necessary, for if there is anything of a swell we could not get out again."

As they approached the place Harry gave a shout, which was at once answered. The sails were lowered, and the boat passed round the edge of the rocks.

"It is a rum place," the mate repeated. "Why, one might have rowed past here fifty times without thinking there was water inside the rocks. Of course you must have lowered the sacks down from the top?"

"It was a difficult job," Harry said carelessly; "but we were anxious to get the things away quietly. If we had taken them down to the port we should have had no end of bother, and a hundred men would have set off at once to try and find out where we got the ore."

Bertie and Dias had everything ready, and as the boat drew up alongside the rocks on which they were standing the former said, "Everything all right, Harry?"

"Yes, I hope so. We are to put the ore on board the *London* tomorrow after dark; she will get up her anchor at daylight. You have got all the bags ready, I hope?"

"Everything the others will be ready for you when you come back for them."

"The next ship sails in about a week. Now, let us get them on board at once, I don't want to stop in here a minute longer than is necessary. There is scarcely a breath of wind now; if it doesn't blow up a bit in the morning, we shall have a long row before us to get there in time. This is my brother, Owen; the other is a mule-driver, who has been my guide and companion for the past year, and whom I am proud to call my friend."

"You don't want anything in the way of food, do you?" Bertie asked.

"We have got some here," Harry laughed. "I am too old a sailor to put to sea without having provisions in my craft. Now, let us get the bags on board."

It did not take them long to transfer the sacks into the boat.

"They are pretty heavy," the mate said, "I should say a hundredweight each."

"About that," Harry said carelessly. "This ore stuff is very heavy."

As soon as all was on board Harry said: "Now we can put out at any moment, but I don't want to leave till dark. We may as well begin to get the rest of the bags out here at once. We might finish that job before we start. Then you could come down with us, Bertie, and Dias could pack up the remaining stores to-morrow and start for Lima with the mules, and his wife and José.

"Very well, Harry. I think we can leave the sacks here safely."

"Just as safely as if they were ashore. So far as we know no one has been in here for the past two hundred years, and no one is likely to come in the next week."

By evening all the work was done. The mate had been greatly surprised at the manner in which the bags had been brought on board, but had helped in the work and asked no questions. As soon as it was dark they rowed out from the cove. There was not a breath of wind. Bertie volunteered to take the first watch, the mate to take the next.

Harry was not sorry to turn in. He had had but little sleep for the past week. Everything had seemed to be going well, but at any moment there might be some hitch in the arrangements, and he had been anxious and excited. Wrapping himself in his poncho he lay down in the stern of the boat and slept soundly until morning.

"I have had a sleep," he said on waking. "I have slept longer to-night than I have done for the past fortnight. Now I will take the helm. How fast have we been moving?"

"We have not gone many miles, and if what tide there is hadn't been with us we should not have moved at all, for the sails have not been full all night. A breeze only sprang up an hour ago, and we are not moving through the water now at more than a knot and a half; but I think it is freshening."

"I hope it is," Harry said. "It is not often that we have a dead calm; but if it doesn't spring up we shall have to row. With two tons and a half of stuff on board it is as much as we can do to move two knots an hour through the water."

"All right, sir! when you think it is time to begin, stir me up."

In half an hour the breeze had increased so much that the boat was running along three knots an hour. By eight o'clock she was doing a knot better. So she ran along till, at four o'clock in the afternoon, the wind died away again, and they could just see the masts of the ships at Callao in the distance.

"I should think that we are about fifteen miles off," Harry said.

"About that," Bertie replied. "We had better get our oars and help her along, she is not going much more than a knot through the water an hour."

They got out the oars and set to work. Occasionally a puff of wind gave them a little assistance, but it was one o'clock before they arrived alongside the *London*.

A lamp was alight at the gangway as arranged, and two sailors were on watch.

"The captain turned in an hour ago, sir," one of them said. "He left orders that the mate was to call him if you arrived. We will soon have him up."

In five minutes the mate and four other sailors were on deck.

"We have got a whip rigged in readiness," the officer said. "How much do the packages weigh, sir?"

"They are leathern bags, and weigh about a hundred-weight each."

"How many are there?"

"Forty-six."

"We have got the fore-hatch open, and can hand them down in no time. If you will pass the boat along to the chains forward we shall be ready for you. Shall I send a couple of hands down into the boat to hook them on?"

"No you needn't do that."

As soon as the boat reached her station a rope with a couple of small chains attached descended. One of the chains was fastened round a bag, and this was at once run up. By the time the rope came down again the other chain was passed round another bag, and in a quarter of an hour the whole were on board and down in the hold. The captain had now come out.

"So you have got them off all right, Mr. Prendergast?"

"Yes. There are forty-six bags. We will say, roughly, two ton and a half; though I doubt whether there is as much as that. At any rate, I will pay you for the freight agreed upon at once. They have all got labels on them, and on your arrival, after being handed into store, are to remain till called for. I am coming on in the *Nancy*. I do not know whether she is faster than you or not. At any rate, she is not likely to be long behind you."

"I think that possibly you will be home first, sir; the

Nancy made the voyage out here a fortnight quicker than we did; but it depends, of course, on what weather we meet with. I was on board her this afternoon, and her captain and I made a bet of five pounds each as to which would be in the port of London first. I shall have the anchor up by daylight. Now, gentlemen, will you come down into the cabin and we will take a glass together."

Harry did so, and after emptying a tumbler and wishing the captain a quick and pleasant voyage, he got into the boat and rowed two or three miles along the shore, as a landing at that time of night might cause questions to be asked; and then lay down and slept by turns until morning broke. A light breeze then sprang up, and hoisting sail they returned to Callao. The *London* was already far out at sea.

CHAPTER XVI

HOME

Two days later, Dias, José, and Maria arrived at Callao, having left the mules at Lima.

"Was it got off all right, señor?" Dias asked.

"Yes. It was pretty near touch, for we had to row nine hours, and only saved our time by an hour."

"And when will you start again?"

"The Nancy sails in four days, so I shall go down tomorrow morning. I don't want to run the risk again of losing the boat."

"Well, we shall be stronger handed," Bertie said. "Of course I shall go down with you; Dias says he will too; so we will be able to man four oars, if necessary."

"What have you done with the goods?" Harry asked.

"I sold them all at Lima, señor, to the man I got them from. He took off a third of the price, and said he could not have taken them if it had not been that he had just got an order down from the Cerro mines, and was short of some of the things they had ordered."

"That is all right, Dias."

Harry secured two rooms at the hotel, and they all sat talking far into the night. "I hope you will get your silver down as comfortably as we have got the gold."

"I have no fear about that, señor. The difficulty will be for me to know what to do with it. I can never spend so much.

"Oh, nonsense, Dias!"

"I mean it, señor. Maria and I are quite agreed that we don't want any larger house than we have got; and I know that if we did want a big one, there would be all sorts of questions as to where I had got the money from."

"There would be no difficulty in answering that, Dias. You told me how your friend found five mule-loads of silver in the bats' cave. You have only got to say that you found yours hidden away, which would be the truth. José is nineteen now, and you will want to provide him with some good mules, and to put by some money for him when he wants to marry and settle. I know you spoke very highly of an institution at Lima for the orphans of natives. You can hand them over some, and when you and Maria don't want it any longer you can leave them the rest."

Maria cried bitterly in the morning when they said goodbye. "I shall love you and pray for you always señors," she sobbed. "I shall never forget all your kindness."

"We owe you more than you owe us," Harry said. "You have always been ready to do everything, and you have kept us alive with your merry talk and good spirits. You may be very sure that we shall never forget you."

José was almost equally affected. "You will never come back, señor," he said, as the tears rolled down his cheeks.

"I may some day, José. I think it likely that I shall some day get up a company to drain that lake in the golden valley. The gold will be more useful as money than lying there. It must depend partly upon whether the country is settled. People will not put money into Peru as long as you are always fighting here."

Maria and José would have accompanied them down to the boat the next morning, but Dias pointed out to them that they were apparently only going out for a day's sail, and that if there were any partings on the shore it would at once attract the suspicions of the customs-house officials there.

Accordingly, after a painful farewell, Dias and the two brothers went down to the boat, where the mate was already awaiting them. The voyage was as successful as the previous one had been. On the return journey the wind held, and they arrived alongside of the *Nancy* by eleven o'clock; the bags were all safely in the hold by midnight. The first mate of the ship had two days before been taken with fever and sent ashore, and the captain had gladly accepted the offer of Harry's assistant to take the berth of second mate, that officer having succeeded to the post of the first. Harry had told him that he could sell the boat, and he had, before starting on the trip, done so, on the understanding that it would be found on the beach in charge of Dias when the *Nancy* had sailed.

Harry had given him another ten pounds to provide himself with an outfit, and had also asked him to distribute twenty among his former shipmates for the same purpose, as these had lost all their clothing except what they stood in. The ship's dinghy, with a couple of hands, towed the boat, with Dias in it, to the shore. The muleteer was greatly affected at parting with Harry and his brother.

"It has been a fortunate journey for us both," Dias said, "and I shall always look back to the time we spent together with the greatest of pleasure."

"Here is a piece of paper with my address in London. I know that you will have no difficulty in getting letters written for you. Let me hear from you once every six months or so, telling me how you are getting on, and I will write to you. Goodbye! We shall always remember you, and be thankful that we had so faithful a guide here, and, I may say, so faithful a friend."

The voyage home was an uneventful one, save that they met with a heavy storm while rounding the Horn, and for some days the vessel was in great danger. However, she weathered it safely, and when she arrived in the Thames she found that the *London* had come up on the previous tide.

"If it hadn't been for that storm we should have beaten her easily," the captain said. "But I don't mind losing that fiver, considering that we have gained four days on her."

On landing, Harry went straight to the Bank of England and informed the managers that he had two hundred and eighty-two ingots of gold, weighing about twenty pounds each, which he wished to deposit in their vaults until they could weigh them and place their value to his credit, and he requested them to send down one of their wagons to the docks the next day to receive them. On the following evening he had the satisfaction of knowing that the whole of the treasure was at last in safe-keeping. Then he took a hackney-coach and drove to Jermyn Street, where he had taken rooms, having the night before carried there the trunks which he had stored before he left England. He smiled as he spread out suit after suit.

"I don't know anything about the fashions now," he said, "and for aught I can tell they may have changed altogether. However, I don't suppose there will be such an alteration that I shall look as if I had come out of the ark. Certainly I am not going to wait till I get a new outfit.

"It did not seem to me," he said to himself, "that I left a ridiculously large wardrobe before I went. But after knocking about for two years with a single change, it really does seem absurd that I should ever have thought I absolutely required all these things. Now, I suppose I had better write to the old man and say that I have returned, and shall call upon him to-morrow. The chances are ten to one against my catching him in now, and as this is rather a formal sort of business, I had better give him due notice; but I cannot keep Hilda in suspense. I wonder whether she has the same maid as she had before I went away. I have given the girl more than one half-guinea, and to do her justice I believe that she was so attached to her mistress that she would have done anything for her without them. Still, I can't very well knock at the door and ask for Miss Fortescue's maid; I expect I must trust the note to a footman. If she does not get it, there is no harm done; if he hands it to her father, no doubt it would put him in a towering rage, but he will cool down by the time I see him in the morning."

He sat down and wrote two notes. The first was to Mr. Fortescue; it only said:—

"Dear Sir,—I have returned from abroad, and shall do myself the pleasure of calling upon you at eleven o'clock to-morrow morning to discuss with you a matter of much importance to myself."

The note to Hilda was still shorter:—

"My darling,—I am home and am going to call on your father at eleven o'clock to-morrow morning. I am two months within the two years—Yours devotedly,

"HARRY PRENDERGAST."

Having sealed both letters, he walked to Bedford Square. When the door opened, he saw that the footman was one of those who had been in Mr. Fortescue's service before he left.

"You have not forgotten me, Edward, have you?"

"Why it is Mr. Prendergast! Well, sir, it is a long time since we saw you."

"Yes, I have been abroad. Will you hand this letter to Mr. Fortescue. Is he in at present?"

"No, sir; he and Mrs. Fortescue are both out. Miss Fortescue is out too."

"Well now, Edward, will you hand this letter quietly to Miss Fortescue when she come in?" and he held out the note and a guinea with it.

The man hesitated.

"You need not be afraid of giving it to her," Harry went on. "It is only to tell her what I have told your master in my letter to him, that I am going to call to-morrow."

"Then I shall be glad to do it," the man said—for, as usual, the servants were pretty well acquainted with the state of affairs, and when Harry went away, and their young mistress was evidently in disgrace with her father, they guessed pretty accurately what had happened, and their sympathies were with the lovers. Harry returned to Jermyn Street confident that Hilda would get his note that evening.

On arriving the next morning Harry was shown into the library. Mr. Fortescue rose from his chair and bowed coldly.

"To what am I indebted for the honour of this visit, Mr. Prendergast? I had hoped that the emphatic way in which I rejected your—you will excuse my saying—presumptuous request for the hand of my daughter, would have settled the matter once and for all; and I trust that your request for an interview today does not imply that you intend to renew that proposal."

"It has that object, sir," Harry said quietly, "but under somewhat changed conditions. I asked you at that time to give me two years, in which time possibly my circumstances might change. You refused to give me a single week; but your daughter was more kind, and promised to wait for the two years, which will not be up for two more months."

"She has behaved like a froward and obstinate girl," her father said angrily. "She has refused several most eligible offers, and I have to thank you for it. Well, sir, I hope at least that you have the grace to feel that it is preposterous that you should any longer stand in the way of this misguided girl."

"I have come to say that if it is her wish and yours that I should stand aside, as you say, I will do so, and in my letters I told her that unless circumstances should be changed before the two years have expired I would disappear altogether from her path."

"That is something at least, sir," Mr. Fortescue said with more courtesy than he had hitherto shown. "I need not say that there is no prospect of your obtaining my consent, and may inform you that my daughter promised not to withstand my commands as far as you are concerned beyond the expiration of the two years. I do not know that there is anything more to say."

"I should not have come here, sir, had there not been more to say, but should simply have addressed a letter to you saying that I withdrew all pretensions to your daughter's hand. But I have a good deal more to say. I have during the time that I have been away succeeded in improving my condition to a certain extent.

"Pooh, pooh, sir!" the other said angrily. "Suppose you made a thousand or two, what possible difference could it make?"

"I am not foolish enough to suppose that it would do so; but at least this receipt from the Bank of England, for gold deposited in their hands, will show you that the sums you mention have been somewhat exceeded."

"Give it me," Mr. Fortescue said, holding out his hand. "Let us get through this farce as soon as possible; it is painful to us both."

He put on his spectacles, glanced at the paper, and

gave a sudden start; read it again, carefully this time, and then said slowly:

"Do you mean that the two hundred and eighty-two ingots, containing in all five thousand six hundred and forty pounds weight of gold, are your property?"

"It is the sole property, Mr. Fortescue, of my brother and myself. I own two-thirds of it. It is lost treasure recovered by us from the sea, where it has been lying ever since the conquest of Peru by Pizarro. The ingots weigh about twenty pounds each. I had a small piece of the gold assayed at Callao, and its value was estimated at four pounds per ounce. Roughly, then, the value of the sum deposited at the Bank is two hundred and seventy thousand pounds."

"Prodigious!" Mr. Fortescue murmured.

"Well, Mr. Prendergast, I own that you have astounded me. It would be absurd to deny that this altogether alters the position. Against you personally I have never had anything to say. You were always a welcome visitor to my house till I saw how matters were tending. Your family, like my own, is an old one, and your position as an officer in the King's Naval Service is an honourable one. However, I must ask you to give me a day to reflect over the matter, to consult my wife, and to ascertain that my daughter's disposition in the matter is unchanged."

"Thank you, sir! But I trust that you will allow me to have an interview with Miss Fortescue now."

"I think that after the turn the matter has taken your request is a reasonable one. You are sure to find her in the drawing-room with her mother at present. I will take you up myself."

Harry could have done without the guidance, for he knew the house well. However, he only bowed again, and followed the old man upstairs.

The latter opened the door and said to his wife: "My dear, I have brought an old friend up to see you;" and as Harry entered he closed the door and went down to the library again.

Mrs. Fortescue waved her hand as Harry, on entering, was about to speak to her.

"Go to her first," she said; "she has waited long enough for you."

And he turned to Hilda.

He made a step towards her and held out his arms, and with a little cry of joy she ran into them.

"And is it all right?" she said a minute later. "Can it really be all right?"

"You may be quite sure that it is all right, Hilda," Mrs. Fortescue said. "Do you think your father would have brought him up here if it hadn't been? Now you can come to me, Harry."

"I have done very well, Mrs. Fortescue. I was able to show Mr. Fortescue a receipt for gold amounting to nearly three hundred thousand pounds, of which two-thirds belong to me, the rest to my brother."

Mrs. Fortescue uttered an exclamation of astonishment.

"What have you been doing, Harry?" she asked—"plundering a Nabob?"

"Nabobs do not dwell in Peru," he laughed. "No, I have discovered a long-lost treasure, which, beyond any doubt, was part of the wealth of Atahuala, the unfortunate monarch whom Pizarro first plundered and then slew. It had been sent off by sea, and the vessel was lost. It is too long a story to tell now."

"And Papa has quite consented, Harry?"

Harry smiled.

"Virtually so, as you might suppose by his bringing me up here. Actually he has deferred the matter, pending a consultation with you and Mrs. Fortescue, and will give his formal answer to-morrow."

The two ladies both smiled.

"If he said that, the matter is settled," the elder said; "he has never asked my opinion before on the subject, and I have never volunteered it. But I am sure he has not the slightest doubt as to what I thought of it. So we can consider it as happily settled after all."

A month later there was a wedding in Bedford Square. Among those present no one was more gratified than Mr. Barnett, whose surprise and satisfaction were great when Harry told him in confidence the result of his advice, and especially of his introduction to the Indian guide.

It had been arranged that nothing should be said as to the source from which Harry had obtained his wealth, as it was possible the Peruvian government might set up some claim to it, and it was in Mr. Fortescue's opinion very doubtful what the result would be, as it had been discovered so close to the shore.

Harry never took any steps with reference to the gold valley, for the constant troubles in Peru were sufficient to deter any wealthy men from investing money there.

The correspondence between him and Dias and his wife was maintained until they died full of years and greatly lamented by numbers of their countrymen to whom they had been benefactors.

Bertie never went to sea again except in his own yacht, but when he came of age, bought an estate near Southampton, and six years later brought home a mistress for it.